"*Hello, Career* is absolutely essential reading for anyone launching a career in today's complicated world of work. Ed Bray is a true expert, sharing the real truth and insider secrets about handling everything from tough bosses to instant messaging etiquette to choosing the right benefits. Best of all, his advice is full of humor and great stories. Read this book—your career will thank you!"

—LINDSEY POLLAK, *New York Times* best-selling author of *Recalculating: Navigate Your Career Through the Changing World of Work*

"While I believe in my academic abilities, school didn't teach me how to 'work smart.' Ed's realistic examples of working smart fill that void. I highly recommend Ed's book to every graduating college senior."

—EMILY FLEMING, senior at University of Redlands, National Honor Society

"Having worked in human resources for over twenty years, I've seen many employees struggle in their new roles because they don't know how to 'work smart.' Things like not understanding the importance of learning our company and culture or understanding the power of a mentor relationship, or demonstrating appropriate workplace etiquette. *Hello, Career* takes employees in their first job on a

journey teaching them how to 'work smart,' putting them in a great position to be successful early in their careers. Everyone in their first job needs to read Ed's book."
—STEPHANIE AYALA, Director, Human Resources, The Michaels Companies, Inc.

"What do you get when you put an easy-to-read book together with essential information to help employees succeed in their first job? You get *Hello, Career*. I really like two things about this book: 1) Ed's diverse working experience allows him to pinpoint how an employee can work smart in any company no matter the size, industry, or where it's geographically located, and 2) Ed truly recognizes and understands the migration from the physical to remote workplace as he shares valuable advice and guidance that benefits employees in either setting."
—HEIDI HENIFF, Associate Director, Human Resources, Crate & Barrel

"*Hello, Career* is a must-read for all employees in their first job. It's filled with lessons and stories that demonstrate the importance and value of working smart. I especially loved the benefits chapter as Ed hits the nail on the head regarding the importance of new employees paying attention to and selecting the right benefits to support their physical, financial, and emotional health."
—ERIN ROMERO, Manager, Benefits, Express

"*Hello, Career* is an easy-to-digest guide to often hard-to-learn career lessons that I wish I had when I started my career! Ed uses storytelling, toolkits, and examples to help those new to the workplace front-load the learnings that often take years to learn through experience. His guidance is grounded in the voice of someone who has been-there-done-that and wants to pass on important life and career lessons, starting with how to hit the ground running through planning for ongoing career development. An engaging and impactful read, I'd recommend it to all getting started on their career journey!"

—ED SOULIER, executive with over thirty years of experience in the retail and hospitality industries

"Ed's book was well-written and an excellent read. His focus on providing practical ways to help employees succeed in their first job aligns with my motto, 'Your legacy is defined by how many people's lives you've touched.' I highly recommend anyone in their first job, whether an office or remote, read this simple and funny yet powerful and impactful book. It will make them wise beyond their years minutes after walking into their first job."

—JASON NEUBAUER, award-winning entrepreneur and philanthropist who founded Affect Change, a worldwide organization dedicated to shifting the way people view giving. His charitable work has been positively recognized by *Forbes, Huffington Post,* and *Entrepreneur.*

HELLO
Career

WHAT YOU NEED TO KNOW
TO BE SUCCESSFUL
IN YOUR FIRST JOB

WORK SMART IN AN OFFICE OR REMOTELY

Ed Bray, JD, MBA

ISBN (paperback) 978-1-7361119-0-1
ISBN (ebook) 978-1-7361119-1-8
ISBN (audiobook) 978-1-7361119-2-5

Published by

www.edbraywrites.com
ed@edbraywrites.com

For every person who answered at least one of "my million questions."

Contents

CHAPTER ONE

Work Smart in Your First Job

✔ As an elementary schooler, did you ever give a gift to your teacher, such as an apple, candle, or gift card, to show how much you appreciated them?

✔ As a middle schooler, did you ever ride your bike to school to help your principal win the district's Walk and Roll to School contest?

✓ As a high schooler, did you ever answer a question to save your teacher from being left hanging because no one else was raising their hand?

✓ In college, did you ever share your notes with your classmates before a test because you had the time to put them together and they didn't?

If you answered yes to any of these questions, which I am guessing you did, these were all examples of what I'd call working smart in school as you demonstrated the keen ability to make valuable and memorable decisions at opportune times. It's likely you benefited from such actions and enhanced your credibility, personality, and generosity, among many other traits, which put you in an optimal position to succeed with those that mattered—your teachers, classmates, and principal.

Imagine if you could garner the same respect and appreciation from your new manager and work colleagues in your first job. The answer is you can, but there's a catch. You'll have numerous occasions to work smart, or make valuable and memorable decisions at opportune times, putting you in an excellent position to succeed, especially early in your career. Here's the catch: school didn't teach you how to work smart nor will directions appear in your employee handbook. So it's going to take more than gift cards and bike rides to propel you up the corporate ladder.

How do you learn how to work smart? Each chapter of this book will provide the answer. Before we dive in, here's how I learned to work smart. Out of curiosity, I'd constantly ask my father about his job and workplace environment (he worked in human resources at IBM for thirty-five years, as did his father before that). Before dinner, at dinner, after dinner, and on the weekends—I considered anytime fair game to question him. Over a span of twenty-two years, he probably answered about half of what he referred to as "my million questions." Little did I know my working smart research had begun.

My dad passed away a month before I started my first job. I was terrified walking in the door as I'd lost my mentor. Who was going to answer my million questions? It's funny how things work out in life because, looking back, I didn't realize it at the time, but my dad shared an unexpected gift with me: being forced to figure out all the answers on my own put me in a better position to be successful.

Over the past twenty-five years, I've had the good fortune of working in ten companies, including leadership positions in Hawaiian Airlines, Apria Healthcare, and Ross Stores, Inc., for seventeen different managers. Plus, I've taught in the University of California–Irvine's extension program and served on human resources advisory councils—experiences that exposed me to a wide range of business professionals.

So instead of counting on one person, my dad, I asked my million questions to everyone and anyone who would listen—managers, colleagues, vendors, family, and friends. No, they didn't answer all of them, but fortunately I found out enough to enable me to write this book.

Let's embark on a journey where you'll learn how to work smart in your first job. Along the way, we'll focus on everything from making friends with the workplace superheroes to writing memorable thank-you notes. By the end of this book, you'll have generated the same keen ability to make good judgments in the workplace as you did in school. In fact, I guarantee those Dr. Seuss *Oh, the Places You'll Go* books accumulating dust under your bed will come to life as you'll be demonstrating to your manager and colleagues you are wise beyond your years and in the best position to succeed today, tomorrow, and the next day.

Tales from the Inside

Welcome to my first book. Throughout it, I'm going to share stories in this section that I've personally experienced in the workplace. Some good, bad, and unfortunately ugly. My hope is you use the message in each story to your advantage as a new employee and throughout your career. Think of each message as a working smart arrow with which you have the ability to hit a bull's-eye every time.

While each chapter includes examples of working smart I've seen prove successful across many companies, some examples won't apply to your company. Maybe you don't have the budget or you have a bad manager or your company culture just wouldn't welcome the recommendation. That's okay, though. I am confident many will apply, and as long as you learn and understand the general concept of working smart from this book, you'll be able to figure out what working smart means for your company, including developing your own examples and executing them successfully.

Thanks for reading the book. I hope you enjoy it. I wish you the best in your career.

CHAPTER TWO

Balance Your Work/Life Seesaw

Have you ever been on a seesaw and tried to make it balance between you and the other person in midair? It's tough, right? Usually because one of you is heavier than the other. However, if you work hard at it and are able to make it happen, even for a few seconds, it feels cool to be suspended in midair, doesn't it?

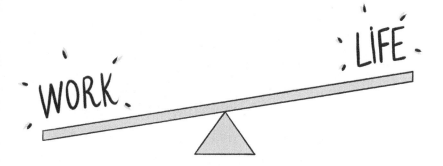

When you think about a seesaw from a work/life balance perspective, I can tell you the weight of your first job (or the work side) is initially going to feel like the heavier side of the seesaw (if it doesn't, you are likely not in the right job). Whether it's the weight of learning the company, the volume of work, the anxiety to complete the work, or the timing to get work done, you'll feel like nothing could sit on the other side of the seesaw to get your side off the ground.

That's okay for a while as it's natural to experience such pressures in a new job. The key phrase being "for a while." If "for a while" means months and even years, your side of the seesaw will start sinking into the ground and that's going to cause you to burn out and likely leave your first job. Let's change that by ensuring your seesaw balance achieves the middle work/life balance we all strive for.

The key to achieving a successful work/life balance requires these two equally weighted sides:

✔ Ensuring you work smart
✔ Making time for yourself

Ensuring You Work Smart

Learning how to work smart is extremely important because, if you don't, you won't have any time for yourself and will eventually resent your company given their lack of appreciation and recognition for all of the hours you are working. In each of the following chapters, you'll learn examples of working smart that, if applied successfully, will demonstrate your value to the company and support your professional growth.

Think of it this way: the harder you work smart, the more time you are going to gain for yourself so you won't be as anxious, you'll better understand what's expected of you, and you'll know how to effectively prioritize your workload. Inevitably, your side of the seesaw will start to rise.

Making Time for Yourself

Even if you work smart, there will always be more work to do in any job. Leave it. Once you've demonstrated to your manager that you know how to work smart, you'll become a keeper and your company will actually expect you to make time for yourself. In their mind, when you make time for yourself, you are clearing your mind and recharging yourself, putting yourself in an optimal position to come back to work energized.

Whether this means going to the gym during the week, spending time with friends and family on the weekends, or taking that two-week road trip to Yellowstone National Park in the summer, make sure that power button is off on both your computer and your work phone, allowing the life side of the seesaw to come to life.

Attempting to balance the seesaw in the middle is going to take consistent effort as each workday never looks the same. One day you are going to be handed a major project the day before you planned on taking a long weekend for your friend's wedding. Another day you are going to get an urgent assignment from your manager as you are walking out the door to dinner at your family's house. The work and life sides of your seesaw will be flying up and down. However, the harder you work smart, the better chance you'll be able to manage these curveballs given the time and effort you've made to ensure your regular workload is under control.

ABILITY to be PRESENT, DEMONSTRATE VALUE, MANAGE WORKLOAD EFFECTIVELY

ABILITY to take CARE of YOURSELF PHYSICALLY, FINANCIALLY, EMOTIONALLY, AND SPIRITUALLY

CHAPTER THREE

Leave Your Schoolbooks at the Door

Know what's going to be hard? Being told to leave twelve-plus years of academic knowledge at the door of your new company. I know you're saying, "Wait a minute. If I can't apply what I've learned in school, I'll fail spectacularly as that's all I have."

You're right. It is all you have. I never told you that working smart was going to be easy. But you won't fail. Believe it or not, you'll actually bring more value to your new company if you put your school learning aside. Let me explain why.

Excited about my first job, I walked through the door and thought I was doing everything right—worked long hours and applied what I learned in school. I even told my friends, "I have this work thing down. I'll be climbing the career ladder two rungs at a time."

But it didn't take long to realize I wasn't being recognized or rewarded for all the amazing work I thought I was doing. In fact, colleagues started avoiding me. Why? Quite simply, I wasn't working smart in my new job. By focusing too much energy and effort on sharing and applying my academic knowledge, I was basically saying to them, "I am doing this right, you are doing this wrong, and here's the best way to do it." Obviously, I was hurting myself and didn't even realize it. As you can imagine, I didn't last long in this job.

Fortunately, my second job allowed me to learn how to work smart during the interview of all places. I interviewed with a senior leader who asked me, "What value will you bring to the company?"

I responded, "Given my academic and internship experience meets the key components of the position description, I think I will be in a great position to provide value-add to the company as I walk in the door."

He looked at me and said, "Nine months."

Confused, I asked, "Excuse me?"

And he responded, "If you are going to succeed here, it's going to take you nine months to understand the company so I'd suggest you put the books and internship experience away for now and focus on learning our strategy, culture, people, demographic, and budget." He then said, "Here's an added bonus. If you understand the company after nine months, you'll gain the opportunity to have a reasonable work/life balance."

Before getting up to leave, he offered one more piece of advice. He said, "As you are learning the company, you are going to see, hear, and experience things that will cause you to say to yourself, why are they doing it this way? It makes no sense. Be careful and smart in how you react. It's appropriate to voice your concerns, but there's a right and wrong way to do so. Don't ever ask, 'Why did you x?' as it naturally sounds condescending and there's a chance whatever you are asking about is meant to be that way. By doing so, you'll immediately drop a few rungs down your career ladder, and if you've ever slipped on a ladder, you know it's not fun."

Speechless, I couldn't believe he was giving me this wisdom.

He went on, "When you see or hear something that either makes no sense and/or you feel you can do better, simply ask your manager or colleague, 'Help me understand?' as this is a nonthreatening way to ask the same why question. Through their response, you'll better understand why the company has chosen to do it that way. You may not agree, but no feathers will be ruffled given the way you've asked the question."

I consider this the best career advice I've received as I've consistently applied it in every new job and it's worked. When I thought the colors for the company's financial benefits website should be blue and green—as I learned in school that those were solid color choices for finance-related information—I checked with my manager who told me that the CEO only allowed the use of the company's colors (red and black) for any company-related website material. When I heard that the company didn't offer short-term disability benefits, even though the company's employee survey showed employees were interested, instead of asking the benefits manager, "Why don't we offer short-term disability benefits?" I said, "Help me understand why the company doesn't offer short-term disability benefits." By asking the question this way, I learned that she attempted to introduce short-term disability benefits a year prior but was told by the CFO they were too expensive.

Taking the time to understand the company is your first example of working smart as you'll be demonstrating to the company that you know it's about them, not you. Making this investment will put you in an optimal position to succeed early on as you'll make a memorable first impression.

Here are seven ways to put yourself in the best position to understand the company when you start your new job:

1: Learn the company inside and out (literally).

You started learning the company during the application and interview process. Once hired, you're in a position to learn more simply by going about your day job. But don't stop there. Why? You've just experienced the tip of the iceberg. To truly learn the company's heart and soul, including its culture and personality, you'll need to dig deeper. Remember the more you learn, the more everyone will appreciate you, so make the time to:

READ EVERYTHING YOU CAN GET YOUR HANDS ON, INCLUDING THE COMPANY'S WEBSITE, INTRANET SITE, EMPLOYEE HANDBOOK, AND ANNUAL REPORT (IF APPLICABLE). Leave no stone unturned. Review and bookmark the company's website and intranet, make notes and highlight key areas of importance in the employee handbook, Google search news articles associated with your company, and view executive leadership's LinkedIn pages to see where they have worked and what they are interested in. These materials will provide a solid initial understanding of your company's personality and culture.

Maybe you'll discover, "Wow, I didn't realize that the CFO was part of the same local financial association I belong to. Maybe I'll meet her at a meeting."

MEET AND INTERVIEW THE HISTORIANS— THE EMPLOYEES WHO HAVE BEEN WITH YOUR COMPANY FOR AT LEAST FIVE YEARS.

(Yes, five years in one job makes you a historian these days.) They'll offer a wealth of knowledge and love to talk about the past, especially the company's highs and lows. This is critically important, as their insight will give you an idea of where you can build on success and avoid stepping on land mines.

Hearing the "I remember when—" from each of them will sound like you are talking to your grandparents. For example: "I remember when the company experienced a major systems integration failure causing significant loss of business. Leadership swore they would never contract to have another systems integration completed without doing at least six months of vendor due diligence."

PICK THE BRAINS OF VENDORS AND CONSULTANTS THAT YOU WORK WITH (IF APPLICABLE).

They may think it's odd you are asking them about your own company, but once you tell them you are looking to learn what the outside world knows and how it perceives the company, there's a very good chance they will be happy to oblige. You might then say, "I appreciate you telling me that the company is known for its long and comprehensive contracting process. I'll make sure to leave plenty of time to review your renewal."

2: Determine your boundaries.

In addition to the company historians, you'll want to speak with your manager and colleagues to learn the company's boundaries. Here's how they can help:

YOUR MANAGER

This person is in the best position to provide insight into what the company is interested in. Obviously, this is important, as you don't want to propose an idea that clearly will not work. Maybe someday they'll find a way to make your idea work, just don't try it on day one. You might hear them say, "I understand your previous company offered a comprehensive well-being program. We attempted to introduce a program that cost $2M last year but the CFO said we couldn't afford it at the current time."

YOUR COLLEAGUES

This will be your trusted crew from day one until you leave the company. Given they're in a position to share everything from "secrets to success" to your predecessor's work tendencies to how to work effectively with everyone in the workplace, be sure to wine and dine them. Not literally, as you may learn stuff you really don't want to know, plus you don't need a call from human resources. Taking them to lunch is a start. As an added bonus, you'll create the opportunity to become friends with some of them (and you can never have too many friends).

An insider conversation may go like this: "Johnny, your predecessor, put together a great analysis on how to communicate effectively with all of our employees. He didn't get to present it before he left so you may want to dust off the presentation and discuss it with your manager."

3: Listen.

In your new job, just listen. Yet listening is hard. Listening is not the same as hearing. Listening means you are actively processing what you are being told. Hearing means you simply heard what someone just said. Think of your favorite class in school. My guess is you listened in that class and maybe just heard in others. Listening shows you are interested in learning, especially as a new employee.

Your manager and colleagues can tell you are listening by the questions you are asking and the notes you are taking. That's going to earn you major points, in and of itself, as it shows you are curious and committed. I've worked with many new employees who talked for twenty minutes of a thirty-minute meeting (because they thought they needed to demonstrate their immediate value), which caused them to miss out on twenty minutes of valuable learning.

Be aware of opportunities to listen as it will be a win for you (as you'll be learning) and a win for the company (as your manager and colleagues will recognize and appreciate your maturity). Listening could trigger your asking a bright question: "Did you just say the company was considering outsourcing its IT function next year? If yes, when do we expect that project plan to take shape?"

4: Take notes.

For a few months, you're going to attend meetings without knowing what's going on. In fact, it will sound like everyone is speaking another language. That's okay. Here's what to do: take lots of notes. If the tip of your pen isn't smoking, then you aren't writing fast enough.

Why is this important? Because one day your colleagues won't sound like the teacher from *Peanuts* anymore and your notes are going to make sense. You'll be in a perfect position to use your notes to better understand the company.

Your notes will go from this: Day 1: "dsafklfa fewfwfw esfjroep dscwfcwrw" to this:

Day 30: "The northeastern distribution center's huddle meetings need to take the FELT approach that's worked in the stores."

5: Ask questions.

Learn the company by asking questions to anyone willing to engage. There's no such thing as a dumb question, so don't be shy. You will truly kill two birds with one stone because not only will their answers assist you in understanding your company's wants, needs, and expectations, but you'll be demonstrating you are interested in developing a positive foundation from which to grow.

See how smart you sound when you ask this: "I heard we are opening four locations over the next year in two new time zones. Should I prepare to change my work hours so I can support all of the locations?"

6: Assimilate with your manager.

Assimi-what? Sorry, I'll lay off the crazy vocabulary. How about this: spending time with your manager is going to be a natural component of your new job, so make the effort to spend even more time with them to learn about the company. Here's why your manager should be willing to make the time for you:

✔ Your manager has a vested interest in your success as you are part of their team. A good manager knows that a key component of your success will be based on your learning the company. That said, they will be ready, willing, and able to help you.

✔ In fact, in one company, my manager scheduled daily one-on-one meetings over my first three months as he understood the importance and value of teaching me about the company before I took key actions in my role. I appreciated his investment of time to ensure I was in the best position to succeed. In fact, dedicating myself to learning the company versus focusing on executing my own knowledge helped me win the Rookie of the Year award at the company's annual event. I then had more good fortune when I was asked to play a lead role in the development, communication, and execution of a new company-wide parent support program to be offered to 85,000 employees in my second year at the company. Given the time I took to intimately learn the company in my first year, I was rewarded by being selected to be part of the parent support program team, which won the Change Champion award at the following year's award ceremony.

As such, take the opportunity to pick your manager's brain about everything. This will put you in the best position to understand the company, including its culture, personality, executive leadership, and staff.

You'll sound like you know the company when you ask this: "Given the different time zones, what time should I send the email announcing the parent support program so that employees in every time zone will receive it during core business hours?"

7: Red flags are freebies.

There's a chance you'll see something in the workplace that doesn't seem legal, moral, or ethical. Could be it's in an area of noncompliance. You'll want to immediately tell your manager about anything you see that is detrimental to you or the company. They will likely take action to address it and appreciate the fact that you made them aware. You didn't need to understand the company to share such information with them.

You could save the company serious legal problems with this observation: "Are you aware that the company isn't protecting employee health data in the way the law requires?"

I'd be remiss if I didn't share one more benefit of making the time to understand the company. You'll learn whether you've made a sound job choice. Your intense research of its culture and values, plus getting to know your manager and colleagues, may have you realize this isn't the company for you. Don't worry about hurting anyone's feelings by leaving sooner than you expected as they know that business is business. Plus, given it's your first job, it's not career suicide. You have to be secure and comfortable in your career decisions, especially in your first job. You don't want the first rung of your ladder to be wobbly.

As you now understand the importance of making the investment to understand your company, taking the time to become aware of its wants, needs, and expectations will put you in the best position to start your career on the right foot. In addition, you will slowly but surely put yourself in a position to determine if any of the school-learned ideas you were ready to apply on day one are still relevant. I bet some are and some aren't.

For the ones that apply, you can eventually share them with confidence to your manager and colleagues. They will be impressed by your ability to work smart (your investment in learning the company from day one) and even smarter (bringing new and practical ideas to the table given the investment you've made).

Tales from the Inside

Tyler, newly graduated from college, just got a call from Manchester Manufacturing offering him an entry-level role in their finance department. After replying an enthusiastic yes, he pulled out his class notes from every finance class he had taken in college and started studying them as if he had a test tomorrow. He was going to be ready for his first day.

During his first week at work, Tyler reviewed the company's financials. Remembering what he learned in Mr. Haggerty's Finance 201 class about budgeting, he said to himself, "Wow! Manchester Manufacturing's budget is putting the entire company at risk as they are spending more money than they can afford."

Which scenario should Tyler choose?

Scenario 1: The next morning, Tyler schedules an emergency meeting with Becky, his manager, and tells her the company has made a big budget mistake and runs the risk of going bankrupt if it isn't changed now. He also sends an email to his colleagues as he knows finding the mistake will make a great first impression with them. He then relaxes in his chair as he knows many thank-yous and maybe even an immediate promotion are coming.

Scenario 2: The next morning, Tyler finds open time on Becky's calendar to mention what he found in the company's financials and discuss the thought process that went into developing the company's annual budget. Before the meeting, Tyler asks the same "help me understand" question to some of his new colleagues so he can be best prepared when he meets with Becky.

Had Tyler opted for Scenario 1, how would Becky and his colleagues likely have reacted? Badly. Very badly, probably. As excited as Tyler is to make a memorable first impression in his new role, he barely understands the company. Therefore, he couldn't possibly know how and why the annual financial budget was determined.

In fact, Becky says to him, "Given the fact the company's budget had been too conservative the previous year, resulting in lost revenue, they knew it was risky but introduced a larger budget this year to attempt to make up for the lost revenue."

As such, Tyler would have learned quickly that while his financial analysis was not inaccurate, it was off-base under the circumstances. Not only would Becky's nose likely be out of joint given Tyler's overly confident approach to the situation, but Tyler just wasted Becky's time by scheduling an emergency meeting that wasn't necessary. Plus, his colleagues, including Marta who presented the case for the budget, would not have been pleased with Tyler.

The lesson learned is this: as excited as Tyler was to make a positive first impression, he failed to effectively balance his school knowledge with taking the time to understand how and why Manchester Manufacturing makes decisions. Had Tyler gone with Scenario 2, how might that situation have ended? Likely, very well. By doing some "help me understand" work with his colleagues prior to meeting with Becky, not only would Tyler have been better informed why the annual budget was developed, but he may have even been able to cancel the meeting with Becky. In addition, Tyler's colleagues would give him kudos for having the foresight to ask them about the budget in a respectful way versus judging them for something Tyler perceived as a mistake.

CHAPTER FOUR

Get to Know the ASPs (aka Workplace Superheroes)

NEWSFLASH: Get to know your workplace superheroes. No, I'm not talking about the ones who wear capes, shockingly tight clothes, and masks that don't really hide their identity. I'm talking about those superheroes who can send

an email faster than a speeding bullet, are more powerful than the fiercest printer, and know everything about your workplace without ever having to get out of their ergonomically perfect office chair.

It's not your CEO. Not your manager. Nope. It's your administrative support professionals (ASPs)—more commonly known as receptionists, executive assistants, and administrative assistants.

Because ASPs are always watching, listening, and learning, plus often report to senior leadership, it's not uncommon for them to have the most knowledge of anyone in the workplace. They know when everyone comes and goes, the details of everyone's calendars, and where everything is, including more coffee cups, important files, and phone numbers for copier repair. In fact, if they could see any better, they would have X-ray vision.

Let's learn how their superpowers can help boost you, your day, and even your career.

They Know Where Everything Is and How It Works

Like any good superhero, ASPs have access to and understand the most powerful tools and machinery. If you're on their good side, they will gladly help you with these often-unforgiving devices. Imagine your panic when the most terrifying villain there is, the copy machine, rears its head in the form of a technological error or a jam—and of course this always happens five minutes before an important meeting when you're making copies of an important document. With advanced knowledge of the workplace's moving parts, your ASP will save your day. Or what about the constant case of the missing stapler? Have no fear, the ASPs know where to find it—even loaded with staples.

They Are Excellent "Guest Whisperers"

When a vendor or consultant arrives at your workplace to see you, ASPs have the unique power to make them feel special. Instead of simply saying, "Mr. Jones will be out to see you soon," they will offer the guest something to drink, point out the restrooms, and ask how their day is. Such interaction can do nothing but work to everyone's advantage as a welcome guest is a happy guest.

They Can Read People's Minds

With vast knowledge of the inner workings of your workplace, ASPs give wise advice. Need to know a good holiday gift to get your manager? You'll learn what treats they can't get enough of. Are you going into a meeting with people you've never met before? You'll learn if these colleagues have more serious communication styles, or prefer lightness and humor. Is your manager in a bad mood? They will let you know, saving you from feeling the manager's wrath.

They Carry Powerful Messages

Remember, these superheroes are not just communicating with you. If they like and respect you, their managers (who are sometimes your manager's manager) will inevitably hear great things about you. Who doesn't want the important people in the workplace to learn about your own superpowers from an unlikely source?

They Uphold Law and Order

ASPs are generally charged with ensuring the workplace looks, smells, and feels amazing. That can work to your advantage, as who doesn't like a clean environment? Careful, though, this power can work to your disadvantage if you are tidy challenged. A little secret: if you are good to them, they'll often look the other way for at least the little violations, like your "illegal" second trash can.

What are the secrets to gaining the respect of your workplace superheroes?

Find Their Hideouts and Introduce Yourself During Your First Week

Because looking for a giant spotlight with their symbol on it might be a bit impractical, you'll want to walk around the workplace during your first week to find each ASP and introduce yourself.

Introduction is not just about a hi and sharing your name. If they get the same information from you that they can get from your work ID, it's not enough. Your introduction should include friendly banter—something light, but not fake. Good chance you'll land on a common interest to discuss now and into the future, like kids, commute, or travel interests. If you want someone to get to know you, showing interest in them will make them remember you.

You can actually start the introduction process early on as you will likely meet the ASPs during your interview process. In fact, a receptionist had the same unique first name as my daughter (we had chatted while I waited for the interview), so that not only allowed us to recognize each other as I came in for interviews but provided an opportunity to form a friendly bond through the entire process. Think about yourself as an origin story. ASPs can help you before you are hired and carry powerful messages to leadership for those they like.

No Need to Stop and Stare— They Simply Appreciate Being Noticed

We all have the instinct to stare in awe whenever we see our superheroes, but, please, for your own benefit, pull yourself together. While their tremendous skills may make them seem superhuman, ASPs are still people, and it's important to acknowledge them just as you do anyone else. You'd be surprised how something as simple as a "Hello, how is your day?" or simple two-minute conversation can create a positive impression.

In every job I've had, I always made it a ritual to stop and ask the ASPs how their days were going, or at least wave if they were on the phone, whenever I took my lunch break. This allowed me to maintain the special relationship with them.

Demonstrate Your Superpowers to the ASPs

It's evident how hard the ASPs work in the workplace. Display your own superpowers by supporting them whenever you can. They will notice and remember as they don't get this "support love" from many.

One time, while walking from one building to another, I saw one of our ASPs pushing a cart full of breakfast (or more like fighting a breakfast monster). Do as she might, the breakfast monster was winning as food was on the verge of falling, and we all know how tragic a wasted breakfast is. This superhero could use some help.

Even though I was heading to a meeting, I pulled a few trays off the cart and helped her carry them to her destination, averting disaster. I was happy to help and even happier when I enjoyed a donut that day and a few others, courtesy of the ASP.

Superheroes Have Bosses Too

Not only should you be friendly and support your ASPs as much as you can, but make it a point to acknowledge all their hard work, especially as it often goes unmentioned or unrealized. This not only includes continual thank-yous but showing appreciation of their superpowers to their managers. I send an email at least twice a year to the managers of the ASPs to let them know how much I appreciate the role the ASPs play as many of us would be absolutely lost without the work they do.

Reward Them for Their Heroics

I've talked a lot about superheroes rewarding the workplace staff through their service and support. Flip the script and make sure to reward them too. The holiday season and Administrative Professionals Day are two appropriate times to do so. Given you know something about them, find a thoughtful gift and include a note expressing your appreciation for all they do. When they see the note includes a thoughtful message, you'll get chills as you'll see a look of gratitude you've never seen before.

Showing respect and gratitude to those truly running the workplace will pay dividends as you'll feel great about supporting an often-underappreciated resource and you'll have a superhero ready, willing, and able to make your life easier and more productive.

Tales from the Inside

Hannah has been with WSB Marketing Consultants for five years. She loves her job 364 days a year. Wait. Why not 365 days a year? She'll tell you that March 10 is a day she chooses not to remember. Ever. Why? It's the day she almost lost her job.

Hannah had started at WSB in March fresh out of college. From day one, Hannah was the definition of busy. Whether she attended meetings, visited clients, or answered emails, she barely had time to eat lunch or use the restroom. While her work performance and job ethic impressed leadership, she barely knew anyone in the workplace outside of those she directly worked with. She was okay with that, though, as she was solely focused on getting her job done and climbing the corporate ladder.

On March 9, Hannah's manager determined she was ready for the big time as she asked her to present WSB's marketing analysis to a top client on March 10 at 8:00 a.m. On the morning of March 10, Hannah arrived at 7:00 a.m. to set up the conference room for the presentation. She plugged the overhead projector cable into her computer but nothing appeared on the screen. Panic set in.

Knowing IT support did not arrive at work until at least 8:30, Hannah darted around looking for anyone who could assist her. After turning the corner to the president's office, she noticed someone sitting in a cube labeled Noah Gehrig, Executive Assistant. While she had seen Noah many times around the workplace, Hannah never formally met him as he wasn't part of her work group.

Sheepishly, Hannah asked Noah, "Do you know how to connect the projector to my computer in the conference room? I keep trying but just get a blank blue screen." Given her stressed look, he promptly said, "Yes," and they were off to the conference room.

Noah pushed a few buttons and turned a few knobs and at 7:57 a.m., Hannah's PowerPoint was showing on the screen.

After the meeting, Hannah realized she had learned an important lesson that day: know, respect, and appreciate the administrative support professionals (ASPs) because they can provide invaluable support during the neediest times. She rewarded her newfound superhero with thanks, lunch, and an email to the president letting her know how much she appreciated Noah's help. In addition, she walked around to every ASP and introduced herself and made small talk.

Now every March 10, Hannah makes it a point to introduce her new staff members to all of the ASPs. They often ask her why, and she just smiles and says, "You'll understand someday."

CHAPTER FIVE

Become
Manager Smart

Remember being parent smart as a teenager? Or said another way, you managed your relationship with your parents in a way that made life pleasant for all. You were smart enough to know the importance of sitting at the dinner table until everyone was finished, and, in turn, they trusted you with the family car.

How did you become parent smart? You learned how each of them ticked and continuously focused on pressing all the right buttons. In the working world, you'll have the same opportunity with your manager as you did with your parents. It's called being manager smart. Add "learning and understanding how your manager operates so you can satisfy them" to your job description as it will be worth your time and energy. The payoff for taking such action will be:

- ✔ Gaining their trust and respect, which is the cornerstone of any manager/employee relationship.
- ✔ Improving your working environment. Learning your manager's emotions (happy, excited, irritated, angry, hungry) will signal how to effectively work with them at any given time. If they're Oscar the Grouch, you'll know to stay away from their trash can.
- ✔ A better likelihood of providing high-quality work as you will clearly understand what they are expecting.
- ✔ Optimizing your chances for financial reward—think merit increases and bonuses, plus career growth in the form of promotions—as you know how to meet their wants and needs.

Now that we've established that being manager smart will enhance your chances for two highly popular payoffs to any employee—cash and career growth—let's talk about how you can make it happen.

You are going to want to learn and execute what your manager deems most important. Having reported to seventeen different managers, I've taken some interesting actions to make them happy—everything from hosting third-shift employee health fairs at 3:00 a.m. to dressing up New Orleans style and marching in our workplace's Mardi Gras parade. Here are four ways you can determine what's most important to your manager:

1. During the Position Application, Interview Process, and First Few Days on the Job

Believe it or not, you started learning what was important to your manager before meeting them. No, it's not because you are clairvoyant; it's because your manager likely developed your position description. This means what's written in the description is what's important to them. Then, I am sure they expanded on what's important to them from the position description during your interview. So, by going through the recruiting process, you had your first opportunity to be manager smart.

Before your first day, take another look at your position description and interview notes so you are well prepared for your first meeting with your manager. This will pave the way for an amazing working relationship as it is likely they won't connect the dots back to the position description and will say to themselves, "How did Paul know that was so important to me? Very impressive." You might even spook them with your mind-reading abilities.

During your first few meetings with your manager, also make the time to shoot the breeze about their personal interests such as, "Jack, what do you do for fun when you're not at work?" or "I'm a cat person, are you?" This will present an opportunity to learn what's important to your manager outside of work. This will help when it comes to determining thoughtful birthday and holiday gifts.

For example, I reported to a manager who loved college football. Because I am very interested in sports and constantly scour sports websites, I often shared information about his favorite team with him. Our interactions opened the door to learn additional personal areas of importance to him, like that he and his wife enjoyed small dogs. Fortunately, I didn't have to go as far as to paint my face to match the team's colors to get to know him better.

2. One-on-One Meetings

After starting your new job, try to spend as much time as possible with your manager. Given your manager is probably running around like crazy most of the day, the best way to make this happen is scheduling dedicated one-on-one meetings. These meetings will provide a great opportunity to become manager smart as you'll have a constant forum to learn and then execute what's important to them.

Here are some recommendations on how to maximize the value of your one-on-one meetings:

✔ Request thirty- to sixty-minute meetings on a daily basis for the first few weeks. This is a surefire way to understand your manager's personality and expectations. Plus, you will learn a tremendous amount about the company in a short period of time, which is optimal to making well-informed recommendations and decisions. If daily meetings are not practical given your manager's schedule, request weekly meetings.

✔ Develop a well-organized agenda for every meeting. List your manager's highest priority items at the top of the agenda and send it to them before you meet. Allowing time for a pre-read, coupled with well-prepared organization, will result in an effective and efficient meeting. Your manager will appreciate the heads-up, and you'll find it's easier to get through your entire agenda.

Here's an example:

Agenda Item: Annual Budget
Description: Need to determine the department's budget for the upcoming year
Status: Analyzing current and expected spend to best forecast next year's budget
Due Date: September 30

Agenda Item: New California Payroll Law

Description: Must comply with new payroll law that will impact 2,500 employees

Status: Meeting with legal next week to better understand the company's compliance requirements

Due Date: October 1

Agenda Item: Andre's 25th anniversary

Description: Plan Andre's 25th anniversary party, including current and past team members

Status: Sent an email to invitees to see which date will work best for everyone

Due Date: October 22

✔ In one of your first one-on-one meetings, ask your manager their definition of success. This is the ultimate "What's important to you?" question. The fact that you have the foresight to ask this question so early in your career will impress your manager, and learning the answer will be like receiving a map with directions to a treasure chest. The more you understand and follow the map (which essentially means you are successfully executing what's important to your manager), the closer you will get to the treasure chest. If you reach it, it's yours (think praise, recognition, bonus, or promotion).

3. Walk or Lunch

Periodically, make the time to go for a walk or have a healthy lunch (courtesy of your physician and well-being program cheerleaders) with your manager with the following caveat—no work topics allowed. You'll enjoy the needed mental break having conversations about mutual interests and family life. Plus, you'll continue to learn what's important to them, resulting in a win/win—a nice walk or lunch and a laid-back opportunity to better learn how they tick.

4. Social Events

This might make you feel like a spy gathering intel, but part of any job that requires social interaction involves observation. Observe your manager at social events. This could include paying attention to what they bring to the potluck, noticing their Halloween costume, or observing how they behave at the holiday party. You're guaranteed to learn things your manager considers important to them that you never knew, whether they like potato salad, enjoy pretending to be a pirate, or are really good at laughing like Santa Claus.

Once you've gathered your intel, execute your plan. For example, if you learn that St. Patrick's Day is your manager's favorite holiday, leaving a four-leaf clover on their desk will surely grant you the luck of the Irish.

In addition to focusing on learning and executing what your manager deems important, you'll also become manager smart by making their job easier. Why? Making their job easier gives them the gift of time, which is arguably the most priceless benefit in the working world. There are a few things you can do to give them this wonderful gift (and none of them include a DeLorean, so please watch the movie *Back to the Future* if you have no idea what I am referring to):

**IF YOU BRING YOUR MANAGER A
PROBLEM, PROPOSE A SOLUTION.**

You are going to run into issues that are unsolvable on your own. The good news is your manager will be ready, willing, and able to help you. That's why they are paid the big bucks. However, don't just drop a problem on their desk and say you are headed to lunch. For one, that's not a smart business move, and, two, you have the fortunate opportunity to earn points for taking initiative and making your manager's job easier. In fact, consider these benefits:

✔ Your recommendation may be the solution.
✔ Your recommendation may not be the solution, but it will likely provide valuable information for your manager to use in formulating the solution.

Sit down with your manager and figure out a solution together. Your manager will thank you as they will now have the time to eat lunch too.

VOLUNTEER TO TAKE WORK OFF THEIR DESK.
During your one-on-one meetings, there's a good chance you'll learn what your manager is working on. If you recognize something you can reasonably handle, volunteer to take the work off their desk. Maybe they will let you, resulting in a win/win—your manager will be thrilled that they don't have to sit in the dunking booth at the company health fair, and you'll gain the opportunity to learn something new, like how cold the water really is in a dunking booth.

SOUND THE ALARM WHEN NECESSARY.
If something important happens affecting your department and you're aware but your manager isn't—like your vendor just called and said they are going to miss their deadline—alert your manager as soon as possible. Don't wait until your one-on-one meeting. They will not feel bothered. In fact, they will appreciate the heads-up. If you wait to tell them, the possibility of everything spinning out of control increases and will likely take more time to resolve it.

If you make a mistake—like you just realized you made a major typo on a presentation you just sent to management—make everyone impacted aware as soon as possible, including your manager. Waiting to tell them because you're nervous you'll get in trouble or think you can fix it yourself will often result in more harm and a longer corrective action process.

Take comfort in this: while your manager may be disappointed in the mistake, a smart manager knows that everyone makes mistakes. So, unless you habitually make mistakes, you don't have to worry about serious repercussions, and your manager will appreciate you told them about it sooner than later as later means they are likely going to have to spend more time dealing with it.

● ● ●

Oh, another chance to be manager smart: their birthday. This one's a no-brainer as everyone loves being celebrated on their birthday (even if they say they don't). So you know you have at least one day a year to further develop your relationship with your manager. (Just kidding. I expect everything else in this chapter will work too.) Unless their birthday is the day after you start at the company, you'll have plenty of time to learn what they are interested in. Knowing what that is, buy them a thoughtful gift each year, whether that's a mug with their favorite team's logo, a gift card to their favorite restaurant, or a sampling of their favorite candy. They will value the fact you remembered their special day and got them a meaningful gift.

By focusing on learning and executing what is most important to your manager, plus doing what you can to make their job easier and celebrating their birthday, you will effectively become manager smart. A good manager will recognize this and reward you in multiple ways, including everything from thanks and appreciation, to making you a trusted confidant, to supporting your climb up the corporate ladder.

All said, while there is tremendous value-add to becoming manager smart, you will want to balance being manager smart against being true to yourself and the unique value you bring to your role. Unless you are a robot or Dwight from *The Office*, it wouldn't be realistic to act like a subservient droid all the time. Hopefully, your manager will see and respect the importance and value of you, as any manager who wants you to conform to their exact expectations all the time is not the manager for you.

Okay, think back to your teenage years one more time. I'm sure your definition of being parent smart was different at age thirteen than it was at nineteen. The same could be said about the working world. Be prepared to recognize and adapt to new definitions of manager smart as you and your manager get older and your company evolves and changes. By taking the actions outlined in this chapter, plus introducing new definitions of manager smart throughout your career, you'll maximize value for everyone.

Tales from the Inside

Reporting to seventeen managers during my career gave me the opportunity to learn and study many distinct leadership and management styles. In addition to the guidance I've outlined in this chapter, which effectively applies to any type of manager, here are some additional tips to become manager smart with specific manager types.

Manager Type: Micromanager

Management Style with Employees in First Job: Micromanagers closely supervise their employees' day-to-day responsibilities so they will certainly keep employees in their first job within their sights at all times.

How to Get Micromanager Smart: While micromanagers often get a tough rap for their extreme level of supervision and control over their employees, having a micromanager in your first job can actually work to your advantage. Given their high level of involvement in your day-to-day responsibilities, use their presence to your advantage by continually asking them questions to better learn the company. By doing so, you'll have a better chance of minimizing mistakes and learning how to effectively perform your role.

Manager Type: Executive Manager

Management Style with Employees in First Job: Executive managers are senior leaders in the company so there is likely a wide experience gap between them and employees in their first job. As such, they are often challenged relating to employees in their first job.

How to Get Executive Manager Smart: Given the years of experience gap between you and your manager, it's likely you'll need to count on your colleagues to effectively learn the company and your role. When given the opportunity, tap into your manager's mind as they are in the top position to teach you how to succeed in the working world and potentially even the company, depending on how long they have been employed with your company.

Manager Type: Busy Manager

Management Style with Employees in First Job: Busy managers barely have enough time in the day to get their own job done so they spend minimal time with their employees. As such, new hires cannot trust in them to learn the company's ropes.

How to Get Busy Manager Smart: You are going to need to count on your colleagues to help you effectively learn the company and your role. However, no matter how busy your manager is, make sure they commit to attending one-on-one meetings and don't cancel them. You will need these meetings to get solid direction and guidance in your role because you'll be hard-pressed to find that manager during the rest of the week.

Manager Type: Bad Manager

Management Style with Employees in First Job: Bad managers are bad for any number of reasons (unapproachable, under-prepared, negative, poor communicator, treats employees differently, and more).

How to Get Bad Manager Smart: It's not worth your time or effort as it's unlikely you are going to turn a bad manager into a good manager. You don't deserve a bad manager in any job no less your first job, especially when you're learning how to navigate the working world. If you have a senior leader mentor, speak with them as they may be able to help, including seeing if there is a different role in the company where you can thrive. If not, your best move is to secure a new job somewhere else.

CHAPTER SIX

Gain Quick Wins

If you've ever played a lottery scratch-off ticket and won, you know what a quick win feels like. No matter how big or small the prize, the thrill of winning brings a feeling of joy and excitement over you.

Same thing with work. Gaining quick wins, especially as a new employee, will make you feel happy, proud, and even accepted all at once. Given I've been a new employee ten times, here are two work lottery scratch-off tickets I've seen pay off as winners in every company.

Initiation Project Ticket

There's a 100 percent chance that a boring, mundane, and tedious project is sitting somewhere in the dark corners of your department that you learned about during the interview process or during one of your first meetings with your manager. It's the project no one wants to touch with a ten-foot pole, and they haven't assigned it to you yet out of fear you will resign within your first few days on the job.

For me, that project has been everything from rewriting job descriptions to filing employee timesheets to going through multiple boxes of stuff left behind by my predecessor. Before being told you have to do it as part of your new employee initiation, offer to own this project. Your willingness to roll up your sleeves will gain the quick win of wins.

Here's how you'll win with your manager, your colleagues, and even yourself:

- ✔ If the project still exists within your department, no matter how much dust covers it, your manager needs it to be completed. By assuming responsibility, you will get a win simply because it's now off their to-do list. Plus, you'll gain respect for stepping up and getting your hands dirty to do a task others have avoided.
- ✔ Your colleagues have made excuses for weeks, months, and maybe even years why they can't do the project. Taking it on yourself will elevate you to hero status with them. Why? Because they won't have to do the project,

and won't ever have to make an excuse about why they can't do it again. Gaining such status with your colleagues early on will pay dividends down the road when you are in a bind—in fact, they may feel they owe you a favor.

✔ As boring, mundane, and tedious as the project is, it's likely to provide an opportunity for you to learn something about the company that is critically important as a new employee. So taking advantage of any opportunity to learn the company, no matter how small, dusty, or grimy it is, will always be a big win for you.

Low-Hanging Fruit To-Dos Ticket

When you walk in the door, you're going to be handed a to-do list. Initially, it will include tasks such as how to get your work ID and directions to the restroom. On day two, as you start to meet your colleagues, your list is going to grow. Then on days three, four, and five, it will start getting out of control. Don't panic, though. Think about fruit. More specifically, low-hanging fruit. Why? Let me explain.

Low-hanging fruit is defined as easy work that produces high-value results. That said, look at your to-do list and determine the high-value responsibilities you can complete quickly based on what you've learned to date. Then get them done. You'll achieve win/win status as you'll be happy for checking off a significant number of to-dos, and your manager will recognize and applaud you for the value you are bringing to your new role.

Some low-hanging fruit opportunities I've taken advantage of include researching and resolving employee issues, like providing accurate pay on leave of absence, and updating the employee handbook with background check information.

It's true that assuming initiation and low-hanging fruit responsibilities will likely create more work for you. Don't see that as a bad thing, though. Think back to the joy of winning one scratch-off ticket (and if you haven't experienced such joy before, now is your chance). Imagine winning two, and three, and four times. That would be unheard of when playing the lottery, so imagine what it will demonstrate at work. This sensation will not only allow you to feel good about yourself, but have your manager and colleagues feeling like they are the ones who won the lottery by hiring you.

Tales from the Inside

In one company, I had the opportunity to gain a valuable low-hanging fruit quick win. I was hired into a position where I was responsible and accountable for the success of the company's benefits function. As my to-do list started to grow, I lifted the hood on employee benefits legal compliance and, based on my understanding of state laws, saw the company was not compliant with some state benefits documentation requirements. I was surprised, as this requirement had significant ramifications for noncompliance yet required minimal internal work.

I approached my manager and said, "Can you help me understand [remember this is how you ask appropriately, not being accusing] why the company is noncompliant with the New York, Hawaii, and California state benefits documentation requirements?"

My manager looked at me with surprise and said, "I had no idea we weren't compliant. Thank you for bringing this to my attention. Tell me more." From there, I explained that the company was exposed to significant penalties from three states. And becoming compliant will not take a significant amount of time and effort as the benefits department and internal legal counsel are prepared to take the necessary actions.

I asked for approval to move forward with managing the state benefits documentation compliance project. My manager approved the project, and within two weeks, we were compliant. The benefits and legal teams were positively recognized by senior leadership for uncovering and quickly addressing an exposed area that could have caused significant damage to the company.

CHAPTER SEVEN

Earn Bonus Points

Remember your parents' reaction when you volunteered to do chores like put out the big trash, shovel the driveway, or rake the yard? Their jaws dropped in amazement, they heaped praise upon you, and they told everyone what you did. It made you feel really good, right? Of course it did.

Guess what? You are going to gain the same opportunities in the working world. Taking unexpected actions will impress leadership and colleagues and allow you to earn

DEAR MATTHEW,

THANK YOU FOR TAKING TIME OUT OF YOUR BUSY SCHEDULE TO MEET AND EXPLAIN HOW THE COMPANY'S CONTRACTING PROCESS WORKS.

WHILE I HAVE SOME FAMILIARITY FROM MY PREVIOUS COMPANY, I KNOW I HAVE A LOT TO LEARN. I LOOK FORWARD TO WORKING WITH YOU.

⁑ SALLY ⁑

bonus points. Before I go through some examples, here's the value of earning bonus points in the working world:

✔ Because your actions are memorable, they will stick out in your manager's mind. This means: (1) It's likely that your manager will tell their own manager about what you've done, and everyone likes being name-dropped in positive ways to senior leadership; (2) Your work will become part of your performance review, which could make the difference between an average and above average review (sometimes the above average review results in more money too); (3) Often, whatever you've done gives time back to your manager, which I discussed earlier is the most valuable gift you can give them.

✔ Such early wins aren't expected from someone so new in their first job, which demonstrates you are wise beyond your years. This savvy move puts you in a prime position to be asked to get involved in projects and initiatives you otherwise wouldn't be asked to engage in so early in your career.

✔ Bonus points will give you a feeling of individual pride and a boost of confidence in your new job. Who doesn't love a little confidence or pride with their morning coffee?

You'll have a handful of opportunities to earn bonus points when you walk in the door of your new job. The cool thing about these bonus points is that they are individual to you, meaning you won't impact your relationship with your colleagues, as no one wants to be branded the kiss-up of the workplace.

Bonus Point #1—Meet Your Local and Industry Peers

One thing you'll learn early on is that executive leadership loves to know what others in the local geographic area and national industry are doing. I say this with conviction, as I've been asked to perform this type of research in every company where I've worked. So I am confident you will too.

I've found the best way to answer leadership's question is by meeting and developing relationships with my local and national peers. The good news is that many are happy to oblige as they are being asked the same questions from their leaders. The bad news is trying to get in touch with them (as they are just as busy as you).

I recommend getting ahead of executive leadership's inevitable question by optimizing your chances of gaining such information. Here are a few different ways you can effectively meet and develop relationships with your peers:

JOIN AND ACTIVELY PARTICIPATE IN LOCAL AND NATIONAL ASSOCIATIONS.

You can find local and national associations affiliated with your functional area (human resources, accounting, marketing, finance, whatever your department specialty) through an online search or by asking your manager or colleagues. The value of actively participating in these associations includes gaining a member list so you can develop a large network of peers, attending virtual and in-person conferences to interact with those having similar business interests, and potentially gaining the opportunity to run for any open board positions, putting you in the position to meet even more people.

CONNECT WITH SIMILARLY SITUATED INDIVIDUALS IN THE VIRTUAL WORLD (LINKEDIN IS ONE SOCIAL MEDIA PLATFORM). Start by performing a search of industry professionals with the same job title as you. Introduce yourself to them through email. Although busy, they will likely respond as they are happy to meet someone who can relate to their world. Because you will be interacting one-on-one with them, ensure you know what you are allowed and not allowed to talk about per antitrust laws (discuss this with your legal department).

By taking these actions, you'll have a wealth of resources in your back pocket, which you can easily move to your front pocket whenever executive leadership asks an industry-based question (for example, in a meeting, someone might ask how an East Coast company might handle that distribution question; you pose the question to your new network friends on LinkedIn and get a quick response from someone in Boston). Managers and colleagues will be surprised when you respond to them so quickly with a valuable answer. I can assure you they will remember it, earning you major bonus points (cue victorious music!).

Bonus Point #2—Find a Mentor

Between learning your company, assimilating with your manager, trying to impress colleagues, and performing your day job, you are going to be exhausted at the end of the day for the first few months, and your couch will become your best friend. However, what if I said dig deeper and find the energy to do one more thing? I promise it will be worth it as you will be rewarded with valuable advice and guidance providing extreme peace of mind (aka the most valuable treasure you can gain as a new employee). So ditch the couch and embark on the journey to find a senior leader, like a director or vice president, to serve as your mentor.

In case you are asking if your manager's nose is going to get bent out of shape if they see you hanging out with a senior leader, a good manager will have no concerns. In fact, they should encourage it as it will support your growth within the company and your mentor's role is not threatening to them as they are simply playing an advisory role. However, you should give your manager a heads-up that you are interested in working with a mentor.

Here's why finding a mentor will be worth the search:

✔ You will gain leadership perspective from someone who has proven their worth within the company. Between learning their style, plus your manager's style, you are in an ideal position to determine and develop your own successful leadership style in time.

✔ You will learn the ins and outs of the company's culture. Given company culture is so integral to everything that's done, learning what works and doesn't work from a seasoned expert will translate into a more effective job performance.

✔ You will gain a security blanket—one even better than Linus's from *Peanuts*. As things aren't always going to be perfect, it's good to have someone to talk to, bounce ideas off, and gain advice and guidance from. Someone with such company respect will be especially useful.

I know you are saying, "easier said than done" as walking up to a senior leader and asking them to be your mentor is intimidating to say the least, especially as a new employee. Let's discuss how to make this happen. You may have met one that you connected with during the interview process. If not, talk to your manager about the employees you'll be interacting with, including senior leaders. Request to meet with them to introduce yourself.

When you meet the senior leaders, attempt to develop an initial connection, whether it's through school affiliation, sports, family, religion, work values, or favorite pizza toppings. You'll inevitably find something that clicks. From that point

✔ Demonstrate your value to them every time you have a chance—for instance, when you are doing a project for them, or giving a presentation where they are a member of the audience.

✔ Invite them to lunch to talk shop. If lunch isn't an option, try to schedule time on their calendar to meet periodically. This will not only give you an opportunity to get to know each other better, but you can pick their brain and sponge it all in. The cool thing is you will always have something new to talk about, because the longer you are with the company, the more topics you will have to engage.

How is this a bonus point opportunity if you are solely benefiting from the value of this relationship? Believe it or not, you both will actually benefit, as I can assure you, the leader you connect with will feel honored you asked them to be your mentor. Plus, good chance they will learn from you too. Call it the bonus points switcheroo.

Bonus Point #3—Send Meeting Recaps

Remember when you participated in group work in school? You were either the one who volunteered to take notes or pulled your head into your turtle shell, hoping someone else would assume the role. I am sure you know where I am going with this. If you volunteered, you've already got these bonus points in the bag; if you didn't, time to come out of your shell as you've got an easy bonus point opportunity staring you in the face.

Whether you attend three or thirty meetings a week, you are going to find every meeting is important in its own way. Often, given employee engagement in the meeting (aka everyone's talking), it's tough for everyone to take good notes. That said, you have an opportunity to step up and offer to take notes for the group and distribute them to the meeting invitees. Here's the value of doing so:

✔ It's your chance to gain respect from every attendee, which will often include your manager and colleagues. Everyone will appreciate it, especially those who hated being the notetakers in school.

✔ Those who did the majority of talking in the meeting will be most grateful.

✔ Anyone unable to attend will appreciate the fact they have notes from the meeting.

Make a grand announcement at the beginning of the meeting that you will assume note-taking responsibility and distribute them to everyone who was invited. Just a word of caution: don't be too good at taking notes, or you will be permanently branded as the meeting notetaker and will never get a chance to talk in meetings.

Bonus Point #4—Show Gratitude

I can hear the first question going through your head: "Shouldn't everyone show gratitude?" Great question. Of course, they should, and many do. However, there's a way to take gratitude to the next level and earn you major bonus points. You'll see how a simple thank-you is a rookie move once you're done with this section.

As a new employee, your first few months are going to be one big learning experience. As such, you'll want to say thank you to everyone who assists you along the way. What if there was a way to make thank-yous memorable? There is.

Let's take a step back and talk about the number one rule for thank-you notes associated with interviewing for a job. You don't simply send an email that says, "Thank you" to those who interviewed you. You write, "Thank you" and include the basis and reason for your thanks ("for interviewing me for the position in your department. I appreciated the opportunity to discuss my qualifications with you. I especially enjoyed learning about the enhancements you are making to your supply chain model and feel my previous experience with supply chain will minimize my learning curve."). Taking this extra approach makes you memorable in a sea of applicants and will often give you a leg up in earning the job. Apply the same approach to your new role.

For example, let's say Destiny in IT helps fix your computer. Instead of emailing her a note that simply says

"Thank you," send an email that says "Thank you, your support has put me in a great position to finish an important project in two days, so I really appreciate it."

Here's how sincere thank-you notes will be received by any recipient:

✔ It will surprise them in a positive way, as it's likely they don't normally receive sincere thank-you notes.
✔ They will know you genuinely appreciated their support.
✔ Given the uniqueness, the recipient will remember the note and you.

As a result of being memorable, you will benefit in at least two ways:

✔ As a new employee, your manager and colleagues will be attempting to determine your character. I can tell you that taking a little extra time to write memorable thank-you notes will pay huge dividends, as your character will shine in an extremely positive light.
✔ Everyone you send a memorable thank-you note to will be more likely to help you in the future, especially when you need it most.

Bonus Point #5—Heap Praise

You stand up in your manager's staff meeting and say to your colleague, "Thank you for coming in over the weekend to help me prep for the committee meeting. I really appreciate it as it gave me ample time to distribute the materials before the meeting."

Your colleague will remember that moment for a long time. Why? Because praise is not given often enough, so when an employee receives it, it feels amazing and will often boost their performance as they'll want to receive it again. And their manager got to hear about something they performed above and beyond their normal job responsibilities, which makes the praise feel extra special.

Needless to say, you'll earn major bonus points from your colleague and maybe even your manager for being conscientious and thoughtful.

You'll find many moments when someone you work with is praiseworthy—whether it's because they worked late into the night to help you get a project across the finish line, introduced a meaningful cultural change to the company, or did something as simple (but oh so nice) as bringing in donuts (and healthy snacks to satisfy the well-being champions). Each time this occurs, make the time to share praise with the employee and their manager. The employee will appreciate hearing it, their manager will appreciate learning it, and you'll appreciate whatever your colleague just did to support you. Bonus points times three!

Tales from the Inside

Jacob started working at Whispering Pine Technology. While he got along well with his colleagues and demonstrated good performance, the same could not be said of his relationship with his manager, Ethan. Unfortunately, Jacob learned quickly that Ethan had trust issues because whenever he presented analyses and recommendations, Ethan would do his own research to determine if the information presented was accurate. Jacob had never done anything to breach Ethan's trust. As you could imagine, Jacob was upset.

After meeting with Ethan and learning he was not going to change after he said, "Sorry, but I only trust myself," Jacob reached out to resources he was familiar with for advice and guidance. Jacob contacted close friends, family, and a therapist that he found through his employee assistance program. Over the next few months, Jacob applied the advice and guidance he received, but because his resources weren't close enough to the situation and didn't know his manager, unfortunately Ethan didn't change. Given the impact to Jacob's psyche and confidence, he ended up leaving the company.

In Jacob's next job at PJ's Manufacturing, he had the opportunity to meet everyone he'd be working with as part of his onboarding process, including Amy, a senior leader who'd been with the company for seventeen years. Through their conversation, they bonded over their mutual interests of hiking and camping. Over the next few months, they periodically got together for lunch or after meetings to talk work and their common interests.

At the same time, Jacob started recognizing his manager, Dan, was favoring his fellow team members over him by assigning them high-visibility presentations and important projects. When he questioned Dan about favoritism, he denied it.

One day, Jacob's frustration boiled over and he resigned. However, when Amy caught word of this, she headed into her manager's office, who happened to be the same manager Dan reported to, and said there was no way Jacob's resignation would be accepted. In fact, on that same day, an investigation was opened into the favoritism claim that caused Jacob to resign.

Three days later, Dan was let go and Jacob remained at PJ's. Jacob went home that night and called all his friends to let them know that hiking and camping saved his job.

CHAPTER EIGHT

Your Work Smart Toolbox

Great news! Much of what you were responsible for in school will translate to the working world. Just as you attended class, you will be attending in-person and virtual meetings. Just as you wrote essays, you will be writing memos and presentations. And remember those countless emails and social media posts? Of course you do. Those old friends will make an appearance too—it's like a reunion for all your old skills.

Now that you are in the big leagues of your first job, the consequences for erring in any of these areas are more significant than they were in school. In the working world, errors can cause serious harm to you, your manager, colleagues, and even the company. To minimize this risk, here are some tools to include in your working smart toolbox.

Technology Etiquette Tools

Let's get one thing out of the way before we explore technology tools. Be smart about what you post on any form of technology (email and social media are examples), as there's a chance your audience, including current and potential future employers, will see it (even if your accounts are private) and judge you on the content, fairly or unfairly.

That embarrassing photo of you from a party with the beer can in your hand looking a little (a lot) drunk, that edgy political statement, or that video of you putting a traffic cone on your head and pretending to be a unicorn are what I am talking about. The simple question you'll want to ask yourself before drafting an email or posting anything on your work or personal social media is this: "Am I comfortable with what my company may see?"

Now that we've established the importance of staying virtually smart, let's talk about technology etiquette tools that can support your efforts to work smart.

Email Etiquette Tool

Guess what you are going to do more than anything in your job? Send and receive emails. So. Many. Emails. Think for a second about anything else you do a lot. I bet you've created efficiencies in whatever you just thought of, because, otherwise, you'd be doing it all day. Let's talk about creating efficiencies in emails because an efficient emailer equals a happy recipient.

BEFORE YOU WRITE ANY EMAIL, CONSIDER WHETHER IT MAKES SENSE TO CALL THE RECIPIENT INSTEAD.

Bottom line: any email runs the risk of being misinterpreted by the recipient. Maybe that's happened a time or two from a personal standpoint. From a workplace standpoint, a misinterpreted email can cause serious unintended consequences, including negatively impacting relationships.

So before starting to draft any email, ask yourself, "Considering the complexity and/or sensitivity of what I am about to write, does it make sense for me to call the recipient instead?" If the answer is yes, pick up the phone. Have a conversation about the topic and follow up with an email that highlights and confirms everything you've discussed. You will be in a much better spot, and so will the recipient, simply because you pushed those number buttons on your phone.

DON'T SEND BAD NEWS IN AN EMAIL.

Bad news, such as an employee performance improvement plan or letting your colleague know their proposal was not approved, does not belong in an email. It should always be communicated in person, over a virtual meeting, or by phone. It's not only the right thing to do given the type of news being delivered but also presents an opportunity for the recipient to better understand what occurred and respond verbally.

INCLUDE THE IMPORTANCE OF OPENING THE EMAIL IN THE SUBJECT LINE.

Provide the importance of opening your email in the subject line. Think about it this way. Your recipient receives many emails, too, and there are only so many hours in the day to read them. So make it easy on the recipient by letting them know the importance of opening your email in the subject line. It will take you ten extra seconds and will be incredibly appreciated, plus you'll stand a better chance of getting a response sooner for your higher priority emails. Here are some examples of degrees of importance you can place in the subject line:

- ✔ *FYI* (you are simply making them aware of something and they can look at the email at their leisure)
- ✔ *FOR REVIEW AND ACTION* (you need them to look at the email and respond but it's not urgent)

✔ *HIGH PRIORITY* (you need them to look at the email and respond as soon as possible)

✔ *IS IT FRIDAY YET?* (no description necessary)

ENSURE YOUR EMAILS ARE DIRECT AND CONCISE. As I said before, no one has time to read emails, which is why you've already made the process easier by providing the importance in the subject line. Now, let's focus on enhancing the value of the body of your email.

Think back to your most difficult English teachers. No doubt they drilled the importance of writing direct and concise essays—direct so the reader learns the message early on, and concise so the readers don't have to read for days to understand the message. Apply the same thought process to emails, as recipients appreciate easy-to-read emails. If you don't, you run the risk that every time you send an email, recipients will sigh and delay opening your four-page novel that isn't clear until page four (if they're lucky). Think *The Poky Little Puppy* rather than *War and Peace*.

INCLUDE BULLET POINT MESSAGES AS OFTEN AS POSSIBLE. If there was ever an email hall of fame, bullet point messages would be the first inductee. Why? They'd get votes from senders and recipients alike, as they have all these readability qualities:

- ✔ Are easier to write and read than paragraphs
- ✔ Stand out
- ✔ Carry the point/message of the email
- ✔ Are easy to transfer into other documentation, like presentations
- ✔ Look cool, especially the round bullet points

Become the bullet point email king/queen, and you'll be on your way to the work smart hall of fame.

PROOFREAD EMAILS (AND ANY ATTACHED DOCUMENTS) BEFORE PUSHING SEND.

It's inevitable. You are going to push send and realize one second later there's a typo. This could also happen if you realize you've attached the wrong document. Your stomach is going to drop as you try the email recall function (OMG *where is it?*) but realize that it generally doesn't work. To protect your emotional health and credibility, take an extra minute to proofread and run a spell check on every email, plus double-check the document you have attached is the intended document. Imagine the impact if the typo or document has the audience thinking one thing versus the message you intended to convey. Obviously, that's not good. For more important emails or ones with a larger audience, ask your manager or a colleague to review them before pushing send. Your emotional health will thank you.

DON'T WRITE AN EMAIL WHEN YOU ARE MAD, AND KEEP NEGATIVE EMOTIONS OUT OF EMAILS.

I can say with confidence you are going to get upset at your manager, colleague, consultant, or vendor. Often, you'll want to communicate with these people via email because you don't want to see or talk to them. However, if you don't listen to any other advice in this book, please listen to this: don't ever send an email when you feel that frustration or anger bubbling inside you. Here's why:

- ✓ Your recipients will never be able to unsee your message.
- ✓ Others may see your message (think leadership).
- ✓ Negative emotional messages are never professional.
- ✓ In the heat of the moment, you may not mean what you say.
- ✓ You run the risk of hurting your credibility within your own company and to whomever you've communicated with.

I've never seen an email filled with negative emotions have a happy ending. In fact, they often make bad situations worse. They are a response to irrational thinking, which is never something you want to convey in your role. When you find yourself upset, call the individual over the phone or virtual technology. However, before doing so, do this:

- ✔ Take whatever time is necessary to simmer down and get yourself back in a rational frame of mind. Squeeze a stress ball. Take deep breaths. Go for a walk.
- ✔ Depending on who upset you, reach out to your manager, a trusted colleague, or your mentor for advice. Ask them how to appropriately react and effectively respond. They provide amazingly professional and rational advice, especially if they know you well.
- ✔ If you have no choice but to email, keep it simple, professional, and short. In your email, request to speak with the recipient over the phone or in person.

Instant Messaging Tool

Imagine if you could text at work. Not only would you be able to show everyone why your friends call you the national texting champion, but you'd be in your comfort zone. There's a good chance you can, because many companies offer instant messaging opportunities to employees. But, the messaging rules of the business world differ from the personal world. Here are some you should take immediate note of:

SPELL OUT WORDS IN YOUR INSTANT MESSAGES.

While your generation and maybe even Mom and Dad understand your text language, LOL, there's a good chance some of your colleagues will not. To avoid any misinterpretation or confusion plus ensure professionalism, make sure you spell out the words in your messages.

BE PROFESSIONAL WITH THE LANGUAGE AND WORDS YOU USE. Not that I would expect you to be anything less, but make sure you remember you are messaging your work colleagues, not your friends. Nothing else to say.

DETERMINE THE ACCEPTABILITY OF EMOJIS AND SYMBOLS. I've seen instant messengers in some companies use emojis and symbols, like thumbs-up and thumbs-down, as frequently as the words they type. I've seen instant messengers in other companies use emojis and symbols selectively for things like birthdays, anniversaries, and special moments of recognition. And I've seen companies discourage the use of emojis and symbols. My advice: take a wait and see approach to using emojis and symbols until you understand if and how they are accepted in your company.

MINIMIZE SOCIAL INSTANT MESSAGING. Inevitably, you are going to make friends with some of your work colleagues. What do friends in your generation like to do? Text. That said, I am not saying not to instant message your new friends, but remember you are at work being paid to get your job done. Getting involved in a full-fledged instant message session with your work friends about what you are doing every night of the week is probably not in your best interest. Your manager, colleagues who don't understand, and big brother (information technology department) are always watching.

INSTANT MESSAGES OFTEN GET IMMEDIATE RESPONSES FROM MANAGEMENT AND COLLEAGUES.

Phone calls can be time-consuming. Emails must be opened and responded to. Instant messages appear on the screen and can generally be responded to quickly and easily. Which one do you think managers and colleagues like best? Here's a hint: employees love time efficiencies. Whether you need an answer to a question before you can wrap up a project or a coworker is asking a question you don't know the answer to, start with instant messaging because it will result in a win for everyone involved.

DON'T LET INSTANT MESSAGING COMPLETELY REPLACE VOICE INTERACTIONS.

Sometimes I'll ask my kids how their friends are doing. I always get the canned response, "Okay." If I follow up and ask when they last talked to them, I'll often get a look like I have three heads. Sure, they use FaceTime periodically, but their primary interaction is text. As I've hopefully demonstrated throughout this book, it's important you develop interpersonal relationships with your manager and colleagues, and you won't be able to do that using instant messaging as your primary means of communication. So don't be like my kids. Make it a point to talk to them, see them in person, or go on virtual technology periodically. They'll be happy to hear your voice and see your face.

MINIMIZE INSTANT MESSAGING IN VIRTUAL MEETINGS.
As a general principle, I don't recommend sending or responding to instant messages during virtual meetings as it's distracting to see or hear attendees typing. However, there will be instances you can help your manager or a colleague during the meeting when you know the answer to a question they've been asked and they do not. Subtly send them an instant message with the answer to make them look good.

Social Media Etiquette Tool

Social media is your life. I get it. Similar to instant messaging, though, personal social media differ from work social media. First, educate yourself, understand, and abide by your company's social media rules. If you're going to tweet, make sure it doesn't ruffle any feathers. If you're going to post on TikTok, you don't want it to end your time at the company. In fact, avoid posting anything work-related on your personal social media accounts and make them all private so only you and your friends can see them (but continue to keep in mind that just because they are private doesn't mean your company won't see what's on them).

For example, Dante and Mike worked in the same position for the same manager for three years at Taconic Optics. Because they worked closely together, Dante accepted Mike's friend request on Facebook. During the company's annual review period, Dante received a promotion. Mike thought he was more deserving of the promotion than Dante and ended up leaving the company. In his frustration, Mike sent Dante's Facebook post about how ridiculous Dante thought their manager's Halloween costume looked to Dante's manager. Dante never thought that photo would make its way into his work walls. Dante learned two lessons that day—don't post work-related information and don't friend work colleagues on personal social media.

Okay, now to working smart in this space. You have an opportunity to be active on social media in a way that benefits both you and your company. Think of it this way, the more the world knows how awesome your company is, the more they will want to work with or buy merchandise or services from your company. Cha-ching!

Put on your virtual cheerleader uniform and let the game begin. Your first cheer doesn't even require any fancy flips or handsprings. You just have to post and/or point your followers toward flattering information about your company on popular websites like LinkedIn. Examples include

- ✔ Company financial results
- ✔ Company-sponsored events
- ✔ Major achievements and milestones
- ✔ Articles written about or mentioning your company
- ✔ Colleague posts about your company
- ✔ Company open job postings

As a virtual cheerleader for your company, you will be working smart as

✔ Management and colleagues will see and appreciate your positive marketing of the company. Plus, the talent acquisition department will be grateful to you for advertising their open positions.

✔ You'll meet and get to know more employees within the company, including executives, as you'll have an opportunity to connect with them.

✔ You'll connect with new industry peers, which will not only support your efforts to answer key questions from executive leadership but also help you throughout your career.

Presentation and Spreadsheet Proofreading Tool

It's likely you are going to draft presentations and develop spreadsheets. Here's the golden rule when creating these documents: always have someone proofread your work to ensure accuracy. Why? As mentioned, this isn't school anymore where a misstatement will simply result in the loss of a few grade points. This is a much more serious playing field because something written with grammatical, spelling, or calculation errors could have significant negative consequences for the company such as a lost deal, a poor reflection of your department, or management angst. Plus, your competency will be questioned, and that's not a label you want as a new employee or ever. That's why the proofreading tool is the most important tool in your toolbox. Ask someone you trust to proofread your documents. Depending on the importance of the document, ask anyone from your manager, to a colleague, to an ASP to proofread it for you. I can tell you from experience that even if you look at your document one hundred times, your proofreader will always find something to correct. In addition to catching typos and grammatical and calculation errors, they will likely make value-add suggestions, including style recommendations and sentence improvements, which is an added bonus. Don't forget to give them enough time to read and review your document. Plus, ensure they understand how much you appreciate their support.

Missed Deadline Mitigation Tool

You've just spent the last twelve-plus years in school, so it's safe to say you are familiar with deadlines. Let's start with the obvious—you understand the importance of meeting deadlines. Like a hero from your favorite movie, you know what it feels like to race against the clock. No matter how heroic you are, though, sometimes deadlines will be missed. Some are within your control (for example, you didn't manage time well), and others are out of your control (for example, you are waiting on information from someone else). That said, there is a right way to miss a deadline and a wrong way.

One wrong way is to ignore the missed deadline and hope no one notices. Another wrong way is to blame something or someone. Then, when questioned, you rationalize the miss by saying to yourself, Big Bird (from *Sesame Street*) says everyone makes mistakes so I can too.

You don't want to take this approach, and here's why. As mentioned earlier, this isn't school where missing a deadline simply results in a loss of grade points. A missed deadline can have serious implications for your company. Outside of the fact your manager will likely be disappointed, there will be downstream negative effects, including these:

- ✔ The recipient will be inconvenienced, as they will not have the information they were counting on at the time they expected it.
- ✔ Depending on how much more time you need, the recipient may be further inconvenienced by having to figure out how to get the information themselves.
- ✔ You'll earn the badge of being someone who misses deadlines. In the working world, that is not a label you want, as it negatively impacts others' trust in you, especially as a new employee.

The right way to go about missing a deadline—even if it's going to be five minutes late—is through proactive communication, honesty, and transparency. Make your manager and recipient aware you are going to miss the deadline before the deadline passes. Here's why this is important:

✔ Your manager may have something up their sleeve you are unaware of to help you meet the deadline given their experience, understanding of the deliverable, and the available resources at their disposal.

✔ It's the respectful and professional course to take. The recipient will likely be disappointed, but they will appreciate the fact you had the courage to make them aware before the deadline passed. This is especially true if your recipient owed the information to someone else, as they will have time to make them aware.

✔ It will give everyone time to determine the best course of action—everything from introducing additional resources to implementing a plan B.

✔ It will show you know how to admit your mistakes, which is difficult to do, especially as a new employee trying to look perfect.

Obviously, you are not going to want to make a habit out of missing deadlines, but by taking the actions just described, you will be demonstrating maturity beyond your years and gain further respect from your manager, colleagues, and whoever was expecting the information.

So just as Mom told you not to leave home without your

lunchbox, you don't want to leave home without your work smart toolbox. The tools inside will make you extremely handy around the workplace to everyone's liking.

Tales from the Inside

Unfortunately, what comes to mind are two big oops moments in my career where I could have really used the work smart toolbox:

OOPS MOMENT #1

In one job, I created a Word document I kept updated with feedback associated with my manager, including areas where I'd like to see him improve. My plan was to discuss these points with him when the time was right. One day I was sending an email to a colleague (who reported to the same manager) with what I thought was a holiday schedule attachment (I am guessing you know where I am going with this).

Within seconds after pushing send, I realized I had mistakenly attached my manager feedback document. While I ran faster than a speeding bullet to my colleague's desk, I was too late as she had opened the email and attachment. Needless to say, I was embarrassed, had some explaining to do, and begged her not to tell our manager.

My only saving grace was I sent it to a colleague versus

my manager. From that day on, I double-check every email attachment to make sure it is exactly what I intended to send. My goof is still a secret between me and my former colleague, and fortunately we can now both laugh at that moment.

Moral of the story: always double-check your email attachments.

OOPS MOMENT #2

My colleague and I were in his office making a call to a client. He dialed the speakerphone, no one answered, and it went to voice-mail. We left a message and then took a few minutes to shoot the breeze, including discussing the client in a not-so-favorable light as this client was extremely high maintenance.

As we were talking, out of the corner of my eye I saw the speakerphone light was still on. I gasped, pushed the speakerphone button to end the call, and lifted the phone receiver up and down at least ten times to make sure it was disconnected. Then my colleague and I tried to reconstruct the accidental voice-mail we had just left: What did we say? How did we say it? What will be their reaction? How do we recover from this?

Fortunately, the client never mentioned what they may or may not have heard on the voice-mail. However, from that day on, whenever I leave a voice-mail on speakerphone, I lift the handset up and down at least three times to ensure the phone is hung up. If someone is with me, they think

I'm crazy, but after I tell them this story, they laugh and say they completely understand.

Moral of the story: make sure the phone is hung up or the virtual meeting has truly ended before saying something you wouldn't want your audience to hear.

CHAPTER NINE

Benefit You

"Your benefits will dictate your success in this company," said one of the wisest managers I ever reported to during my first week of employment. Puzzled, I asked, "What do you mean?"

"Think about it," she said, "if you are physically, financially, and emotionally healthy, you'll be in the best position to optimize your work performance. Selecting the right benefits to support your health will put you on the path to success."

That night I put my feeling of healthy invincibility aside, studied my benefits guide, and enrolled in the benefits I was confident would protect my health. She was right about having this peace of mind. I was able to focus on learning the company and my role versus wondering if I was saving enough for retirement or where I'd get the money to pay for my unexpected appendectomy two months into my new job.

As a Certified Benefits Geek (no, that's not an official title, and, yes, I made it up), I'm going to go overboard in this chapter to show you the value of those proverbial flotation devices called employee benefits not only for new employees, but also for employees who have been with the company for a while as well. By the end of this chapter, you may not be able to recite your benefits plan as well as a Coldplay song, but you'll understand the importance of paying attention to your benefits opportunities and engaging as warranted throughout your career. Think about this chapter as your shot of benefits espresso.

New Hire Benefits

Whether your company hosts an in-person or virtual benefits orientation or simply emails you a benefits enrollment guide, understanding your benefits options should be a priority, even if you are still on your parents' health insurance plan or you think being young and healthy means you are invincible and don't need benefits. Here's why:

Your first job is going to be physically, emotionally, and financially tough. There's no reason to sugarcoat it. Your first job is going to be a major change in your life. It's going to introduce physical, mental, and financial challenges, whether that means getting used to a commute, moving out of your parents' house, or having to pay rent. It's critical you stay healthy and on top of your game so you can maintain your sanity and be productive at work. Here's some good news. Help is available in the form of company benefits that support your physical, emotional, and financial health.

Here are the most popular benefits I've seen younger employees enroll in to their healthy advantage:

THE NO-BRAINER THREE

No, I'm not talking about the Three Stooges, I'm talking about medical, dental, and vision insurance—benefits that protect your physical, financial, and emotional health. Unless you are enrolled in these benefits through your parents' plan and you know they offer comparable coverage, it's worth the cost to enroll in them. Why? Because you are not going to get ahead if you're sick (and odds are you will get sick), have gnarly teeth, or can't see your monitor. Protect yourself (and your manager and colleagues), as it's not in your best interest to avoid the doctor, and emergency medical, dental, and vision costs can get very expensive without insurance.

HEALTH SAVINGS ACCOUNT (HSA)

If your company offers a high-deductible health plan (HDHP) as a medical insurance option, there's a good chance they will offer an HSA alongside it. This benefit deserves a drumroll. Why? Because it has amazing tax-saving benefits. Get this: a health savings account allows you to contribute pretax dollars, gain pretax earnings, and withdraw your money tax-free. You can use your withdrawals to pay for qualified medical expenses such as deductibles, coinsurance, and copayments. If you've ever been in the hospital for any reason, you'll know that any little bit helps.

The best part is that you own the account, not the company, so you can take it with you when you leave, which is more than you can say for even a pen or stapler. This is why it's commonly referred to as a medical 401(k) benefit. You can either use HSA dollars now or save them for retirement when you are likely to have more medical expenses. As such, if you are comfortable participating in an HDHP, which I encourage you to research given the high-deductible component, an HSA is one of the best financial benefits offered to you.

As an aside, most companies offer a benefit similar to an HSA called a health flexible account, which also offers the opportunity to reduce your taxable income to pay for qualified health expenses.

It will be worth your time to ask human resources for more information about HDHP/HSA and health flexible spending accounts, including the pros and cons, if both are offered.

MENTAL STABILITY

The employee assistance program (EAP) is one of the best benefits available to you. Why? Because as a new employee, you are going to be anxious, tired, excited, or likely all three over your first few months. There's a good chance your company's EAP will provide some free visits for you to see a licensed therapist each year—either in person or through virtual technology. Having someone to talk to will be powerful to your psyche and even reenergize you. Take advantage of these sessions. If you'd like to continue after your free visits end, see if your therapist is covered under your medical insurance plan. If not, explore visiting a different therapist using your in-network medical insurance benefits.

Your EAP may also offer a referral service that can help you find reputable services, such as real estate agents, education resources, retirement planning, elder care, special needs services, and more. This is a very valuable peace of mind opportunity, especially if you are new to a geographic area.

DISABILITY BENEFITS

While you may think you are superhuman, non-job-related injuries and illnesses happen, and when they do, you'll want to ensure you have benefits in place to get paid as you recover. Just think, rent or mortgage payments, food, and Netflix. Enter short-term and long-term disability benefits. In a nutshell, short-term disability will generally provide a percentage of your salary during your recovery, up to a maximum disability payment period. If you are disabled beyond the short-term disability payment period, you may become eligible for long-term disability, which will generally provide a percentage of your salary during your disability period up to age sixty-five. Check with your company to see if they provide these benefits to you for free as some do. If not, look into enrolling in them to achieve financial peace of mind. On a side note, your state may provide short-term disability benefits. Ask your human resources department for information about short-term and long-term disability benefits.

RETIREMENT NEST EGG

Chances are you will be offered a retirement plan at your job, often in the form of a 401(k) plan. As a young employee you have what's called time value of money on your side, plus you have the opportunity to make pretax contributions and may receive a company match (that means free money). As this equates to dollar signs all around, I encourage you to reach out to your company's retirement plan administrator to better understand the plan and its terms. It will be worth your time.

If you think your budget can't handle a retirement plan deduction, find a way, even if you only contribute 1 percent of your salary. If my math is correct, 1 percent gets you something and 0 percent gets you nothing. Look at it this way: the younger you start contributing, the earlier chance you have of retiring. I know you've barely stepped foot into the working world, but trust me, you will soon look forward to retiring someday.

IF YOU LOOK HARD, YOU'LL STRIKE BENEFITS GOLD.

Sure, you've heard of medical, dental, and vision benefits, but if you take time to study all the benefits available, you'll find at least one that will plant a big smile on your face. I playfully refer to these as holiday benefits because of the priceless looks on employees' faces just when they learn about these value-add benefits they didn't know existed.

Some of the benefits I've seen fall into this category are prepaid legal benefits ("I can get a will completed at no cost?"), pet insurance ("I can get Mr. Scruffy that surgery he needs?"), pretax commuter benefits ("I can save money on my train tickets?"), and an employee discount program ("I can get discounted tickets to Disney World?"). If you want to experience this yourself, start mining now.

THE BENEFITS ENROLLMENT OPPORTUNITY DOESN'T LAST FOREVER.

If you don't make benefits a priority, you'll miss the enrollment boat (which is usually thirty days after you become eligible for benefits, but check with the human resources department), which means you'll likely have to wait for open enrollment to enroll for the following year. Sorry, given this is legally regulated, there are no life preservers on board. Given this information, it's in your best interest to review your benefits options as soon as you are eligible. Just a reminder, this isn't college. Make sure you leave more time than the night before your benefits enrollment due date to "study" your benefits because you won't get an extension from your human resources department.

Everything I just said made sense, right? Nope. I get it. Benefits are daunting, confusing, and complex on their face. Throw in benefits acronyms such as PPO, HMO, HIPAA, ERISA, COBRA, and understanding employee benefits can get downright nuts. Let's talk about who's in the best position to help you make sense of all this benefits jargon.

Given the fact I've worked in eight human resources departments, I can assure you that someone in HR is ready, willing, and able to assist you. So even if you dozed a little in the benefits orientation, they will forgive you and make sure you are aware of and understand the company's benefits. Why? They have a vested interest in making sure you understand your benefits because enrolling in benefits that aren't a good fit for you and your family means

✔ They'll have to deal with your questions/complaints all year because you won't be able to change them until the next annual benefits open enrollment, and

✔ Company benefits costs may increase because you aren't using the plans you've enrolled in correctly.

Bottom line: Human resources is a support function designed to assist so you can focus on your day job. Don't be shy, call or email them. They're waiting to hear from you. Additionally, your company may offer a virtual benefits enrollment decision support tool. In simplest form, this tool asks you a series of questions about your interests, financial tolerance, and expected plan usage. It then lets you know which health insurance plans are most appropriate for you and your family based on your answers. It's like a BuzzFeed quiz, but for benefits. Given the number of health insurance plans generally available in a company, plus the difficulty in making sense of all the different plans, decision support tools can be very attractive and valuable to employees. Ask your human resources department if the company offers a benefits decision support tool.

Investing the time to explore and enroll in the right benefits will put you in an optimal position to be physically, financially, and emotionally healthy, thus enhancing your work performance. Plus, with the right benefits package, you'll have peace of mind that you are adequately protected now and into the future. Lastly, your human resources department will thank you.

Life Happens Benefits

Life is going to happen while you're at your new job. You may get married, have a baby, or buy a house. This isn't the Game of Life, it's the real thing. Remember the medical, dental, and vision insurance benefits you signed up for when you were first hired? They're likely not enough anymore. You'll lose your healthy edge if you leave your new hire benefits on cruise control (in other words, you need to pay attention to your options and update your benefits as life happens).

If you experience a qualifying life event—such as getting married or having a baby—it's generally a no-brainer to add your new family member to medical, dental, and vision insurance, but don't stop there. It's important to review the other benefits available, as some may be new to the company since you last looked or be more relevant with the new addition to your life. Also, make sure you ask the human resources department how long you have to enroll in them after you experience your qualifying life event. I've personally seen employees turned away from adding their newborn to benefits because they missed the enrollment due date, and it's always an unfortunate and uncomfortable experience.

All of a sudden, life insurance might seem important. For example, you may not have enrolled in life insurance when you were first hired because you didn't have a beneficiary to leave the payout, but now that you are married with rent or a mortgage, you'll want to reconsider this benefit to ensure your partner is financially protected. You may not have enrolled in a dependent care flexible spending account (an opportunity to use pretax dollars to pay for eligible childcare expenses), but it may be valuable if junior is entering day care.

Outside of enrolling in benefits as a new employee or enrolling in or changing your benefits when you experience a qualifying life event, annual open enrollment is another opportunity to enroll in or change your benefits for the upcoming year. Take ample time each year to review the available opportunities. Why? Because there's a good chance the benefits you need to support your overall health will be different from the year before. Keep that healthy edge—both for your own sake and for the sake of your family (plants and goldfish included).

Tales from the Inside

Antonio was twenty-four when he started with Geno's Accounting in January as a full-time accountant. While he was offered benefits, including medical, dental, and vision insurance, he didn't pay much attention in benefits orientation as he knew he was enrolled on his parents' plan—plus he had a feeling of youthful invincibility.

Antonio's new job kept him busy at least nine hours a day, including some weekends. Guess that's what happens when you start a job as an accountant during tax season. Guess what also happens? By working nonstop, Antonio had a greater chance of getting mentally and physically sick. Unfortunately, Antonio got the flu, which became pneumonia, and he spent two weeks in the hospital. Not only did he miss delivering his first major presentation, which would have given him exposure to senior leadership, but he didn't get paid for the two-week period he was off work. In addition, he got quite the call from his mom and dad when the expensive hospital bill arrived in their mailbox.

Upon returning to work, Antonio called the human resources department to enroll in benefits but was told he missed the enrollment window and would have to wait until open enrollment in November to enroll for the following year.

Rewind the tape. This time let's see what Antonio could have done differently and how that may have been a wiser decision.

Antonio was twenty-four when he started with Geno's Accounting in January as a full-time accountant. While Antonio knew he was covered under his parents' medical, dental, and vision benefits, the human resources manager encouraged him to read through the company's benefits materials to see what was available to him during benefits orientation. Knowing he had a deadline of thirty days to enroll in benefits, he asked his parents to send their benefits materials to him. Antonio then met with a human resources representative to compare his parents' medical, dental, and vision benefits to the company's offerings.

While recognizing his parents had richer dental and vision benefits, he learned that his parents' medical benefits weren't as comprehensive and, therefore, could become very expensive if something serious happened to him. Knowing this, coupled with recognizing the tremendous volume of work on his desk would likely make anyone sick, he decided to enroll in the company's medical insurance benefit.

In addition, Antonio signed up for the company's short-term disability benefit, which provided a percentage of his salary if he was injured or became ill and needed to be off work for an extended period of time. This was important financial protection to Antonio because he lived in an apartment with rent and utility bills. Antonio knew the value of protecting his health. He periodically visited the doctor for his preventive care exams and annual flu shot. While he got sick every once in a while, it didn't negatively impact his work performance nor his wallet as his doctor bills were generally free or a reasonable copayment.

Moral of the story: Don't be the first Antonio. Review your benefits materials and enroll in the benefits that will provide you physical, financial, and emotional protection.

Key Benefits Questions to Ask Human Resources

Now that you've learned the importance of being aware of and knowledgeable about the benefits available to you, here are some questions you'll want to ask human resources if they aren't addressed during benefits orientation or in the benefits enrollment materials you receive.

✔ Am I eligible for the company's benefits? If yes, which benefits and when? Are my family members eligible for the company's benefits? If yes, which family members?

✔ How long do I have to enroll once I am eligible for benefits? If I don't enroll in benefits by the deadline, when is my next opportunity to enroll?

✔ How do I enroll in benefits?

✔ What medical, dental, and vision benefits are available to me and my family? Where can I learn more about each specific medical, dental, and vision plan?

✔ What additional benefits are available to me and my family? Where can I learn more about each of the additional benefits?

✔ If not specifically mentioned in the benefits orientation or enrollment materials, ask whether the following benefits are available to you and your family:

- Health savings account (HSA)

- Health reimbursement arrangement (HRA)

- Health and dependent care flexible spending accounts (FSA)
- Critical illness benefits
- Hospital indemnity benefits
- Short-term disability
- Long-term disability
- Life insurance
- Employee, spouse, and child supplemental life insurance
- Accidental death and dismemberment insurance
- Employee assistance program
- Pretax commuter benefit
- Pet insurance
- Auto and home insurance
- Identity theft insurance
- Employee discount program
- Retirement benefits (such as a pension plan, 401(k))

✔ Where can I learn more about these benefits?

✔ Does the company pay for any benefits offered to me and my family? If yes, which benefits?

✔ Where can I add or change my life insurance beneficiaries?

✔ Does the company offer any meetings or consultations that will help determine which benefits are most appropriate for me and my family?

- ✔ Do you have a benefits decision support tool that will help me determine which benefits are most appropriate for me and my family?
- ✔ Do you offer a well-being program for me and my family? Where can I get more information about the program?
- ✔ Whom can I contact if I have questions about my benefits?
- ✔ When can I make changes to my benefits? How do I make changes to my benefits?

CHAPTER TEN

Establish Your Inner Circle

You can never have too many F*R*I*E*N*D*S. Cue the upbeat music, the quick claps, and dancing in the fountain. We all want that smart friend, that optimistic friend, that cool friend, and that logical friend. The list goes on and on. Why are these different kinds of friends so important? Because you never know when you are going to need a

helping hand, shoulder to lean on, or wise mind to help you get through life.

The same goes for work. You can never have too many appropriate colleagues in your inner circle. Why? Same reasons. You never know when you are going to need a guiding hand, comforting shoulder, or rational mind to support you in the workplace.

Building your inner circle is a science and an art. It's a science because this crew will include employees with special character traits that complement you. It's an art because you'll want to ensure the right members are in your circle. Get excited, as once your inner circle is established, you'll have assembled your very own work superhero team who will help you power through each day.

To do it right it's going to take time and patience. Yes, you'll want allies as soon as you walk in the door, but I don't think walking up to someone on day one and asking, "Will you be in my inner circle?" or writing a note with the option to circle "Yes" or "No" is the way to go about it. In fact, if this is your approach, you'll likely get at least one raised eyebrow and many nos.

Here's an easier and more appropriate way to recruit your inner circle:

✔ During one of the first meetings with your manager, ask them for a list of all the employees you'll be working with at one point or another. Then informally drop by their workspace or schedule an in-person or virtual technology meet and greet with each potential inner circle member. Talk about what they do and how you'll work together, plus ask about their personal life (such as family, interests, and hobbies).

Through what you learn, coupled with the personal connection you may or may not establish, you will start to get a sense of who belongs in your inner circle. For some employees, you may immediately say to yourself they're in based on the fact that you clicked right away. For others, you may want to delay your decision until you learn more about them.

Before we start talking about who belongs in your inner circle and why, let's talk about someone who doesn't belong in your inner circle: your manager. It goes without saying that it will be important to have a positive working relationship with your manager, but it should be different from an inner circle relationship. Think of it this way. You love your family and your friends, but you have a different relationship with both of them. I've discussed maximizing your positive relationship with your manager in a previous chapter.

Without further ado, introducing the members of your inner circle:

✔ **The ASPs:** As I talked about earlier in the book, you will want to align yourself with these superheroes for a million reasons. Get started on this relationship before you are hired.

✔ **The company historians:** The company historians (employees who have been with the company more than five years) are positioned to keep you out of trouble and lead you to success. Like any guru, they will steer you in the right direction, avoiding pitfalls and land mines along the way.

✔ **Your mentor:** Your mentor is going to show you the ropes, keep things real, and be there when you need them most.

✔ **The human resources specialist:** Having worked in human resources for twenty-five years, I can attest that aligning yourself with someone you click with in human resources will allow you to accomplish big things. Your HR buddy will look out for your physical, emotional, and financial health (you could say that they are a great *human* resource).

✔ **The information technology (IT) whiz:** Technology constantly breaks or is interrupted and IT Help Desk queues are long, especially if a significant number of employees work remotely. Make a friend in IT who has the status and pull to get you what you need whenever you need it.

✔ **Funny colleague:** Work will be stressful at times. You'll have approaching deadlines, frustrating colleagues, and confusing expectations. Having a comedian in your inner circle will make these times better. Laughter is the best medicine, so knowing someone who will crack jokes is like having a medic to take your mind off the stresses of work.

✔ **Colleagues from departments you commonly work with ("Insiders"):** These insiders are your aces in the hole, or your very own secret advantage. By establishing these relationships, you will never walk into a situation blind as you'll have each other's backs. For example, if finance is about to share some bad news with your department, it would benefit you to have a finance insider to inform you beforehand so you have time to prepare for such news. Or if you're working on a big project for marketing, your marketing insider will be happy to share exactly what marketing leadership is looking for. This will put you at a great advantage to meet their expectations. Given this opportunity, you will want to develop trusted insider relationships with colleagues in the different departments you work with.

✔ **Colleagues with similar outside interests:** Who wants to talk about work all day? Not me. I want to talk about sports. Spending time with colleagues with similar outside interests will not only allow you to take your mind off work for a while, but will also give you the benefit of a personal relationship. Having common outside interests with someone puts you in a perfect position to have fascinating conversations, share opinions and ideas, and potentially meet outside of work to do whatever you both are interested in.

✓ **Mailroom staff:** Almost all mail is virtual these days. Key word being *almost*. There are some documents that haven't made their way to the virtual world yet. As we all know, there will be times when you need to get mail out and receive mail as soon as possible. Develop a relationship with whoever is responsible for mail delivery and pickup because you'll stand a better chance of getting their attention when necessary. A nice delivery of holiday goodies to them generally makes you memorable.

✓ **Maintenance staff:** Inevitably, you are going to need something to perform your job that falls outside of your ASP's superpowers. Now, think for a second about handy people in general. They are usually booked up for weeks. That's likely the same for your work maintenance staff. As such, it's in your best interest to get to know the maintenance staff because it may mean the difference between sitting on a chair with three legs for two hours versus three days. When you see them around the office, acknowledge them and put them on your holiday card list to show them how much you appreciate what they do for the office.

✓ **Janitorial staff:** Just as the receptionists and administrative professionals often get overlooked, the same holds true for the janitorial staff. Change that narrative, as my guess is that you are happy to see toilet paper in the bathroom, enjoy having your trash emptied, and appreciate coming into a well-vacuumed workspace. That said, treat these people with respect and dignity. Say hi, ask how their day is, or hold the door when you see them coming down the hall with a cart. They will certainly appreciate it, and you increase the chances that your desk will sparkle a little brighter.

✔ **Cafeteria staff (if applicable):** As you'll constantly be busy and hungry, this is the team you want on your side. The more they know you, the better they are going to take care of you. That means getting your lunch a little quicker (which is a huge help when you are bouncing between meetings), a few extra chips (who doesn't like a few more of any food), and keeping the cafeteria open a little longer (which will serve you well if you get out of a meeting right before the cafeteria closes). Strike up a conversation about anything and everything as they prepare your food or while you're waiting to pay. Food dividends, after all, are the tastiest dividends.

While I've seen the aforementioned individuals most commonly in inner circles, additional staff members could be part of your inner circle depending on whom you work with. That said, here are other individuals that could be part of your circle: onsite nurse, parking staff, facilities staff (especially if you live in an area with snow), and well-being team.

You'll want to treat your inner circle like you treat your close friends. This means it's important you do the following:

✔ **Mentally support one another:** Workdays can be long and challenging. Knowing that your inner circle is an instant message, email, virtual call, phone call, or two cubicles away will provide you the peace of mind to get through the toughest times. Plus, playing the same role for them is very fulfilling.

✔ **Help each other:** Because you work closely with everyone in your inner circle, there will be many opportunities to help each other. Whether that means giving a heads-up so your colleagues can adequately prepare for what's coming or helping someone print and stuff 1,000 envelopes by noon, the feeling of helping and being helped by others will give you a sense of purpose.

✔ **Protect each other:** Unfortunately, work isn't going to be drama-less. There will be tension. When you or a colleague find yourself in the middle of conflict, it will be reassuring to know that your inner circle is there to provide great advice and guidance and have your back.

✔ **Have fun:** Given the amount of time you spend with your inner circle, coupled with the fact you specifically selected them, there's a good chance you will get to like each other. This will likely lead to group lunches, dinners, events, happy hours, and maybe even a spontaneous adventure to stop an evil villain from robbing a bank. Whatever your activity, it will allow you to benefit personally and professionally, and you'll enjoy looking back on the pictures and videos associated with this superhero team someday.

Tales from the Inside

You're leading an important meeting with Breanna, your company's marketing consultant, at 1:00 p.m. However, after an unexpected delay in getting your order, you're still at Paul's Pizza and it's 1:02. You're five minutes away from the office. Inner circle activate.

- ✔ Text to Aisha, your colleague in marketing who is attending the meeting: "Can you please show Breanna into the conference room, offer her water, and point out the restrooms? I will be there in five minutes."
- ✔ Text to Xavier, your fishing friend in IT: "Can you please grab my laptop from my office and connect it to the projector in Conference Room 21? Thanks!"
- ✔ Text to Juan in human resources whom you meant to talk to before the meeting as he used to work with Breanna when he was in marketing: "I'm meeting with Breanna about her company's marketing support services. Knowing you've worked with her before, is there anything I should specifically focus on or avoid? Thanks!"

- ✔ To Emily, the receptionist, as you run in the door: "Thank you for making my guest feel comfortable in my absence."
- ✔ To Ryan, from the cafeteria, as you see him walking out of the conference room as you are walking in: "Thank you for delivering everything right before the meeting started [as the pastries and coffee will be warm]!"
- ✔ Email to Maria, a colleague from Strategic Sourcing, after the meeting: "I understand you shared a few jokes (albeit at my expense) with Breanna while I was delayed. Thanks for having my back."

Mission accomplished. Great job, inner circle.

CHAPTER ELEVEN

Develop Yourself (and Your Company)

Guess what? There's a world outside your company's four walls. It's called earth and it has four seasons and a bunch of time zones. Okay, I know you knew that. But after being chained to your desk and grinding away in your new job, I just wanted to make sure. Now, let me tell you a little secret. If you can manage to sneak out of those four walls

periodically, which could mean literally leaving the office or your remote work environment or simply making the time to attend virtual events, you can bring back some amazing wins for you and your company. I know you're probably thinking that any reason to leave the office would have to be really important. How can you afford to miss the monthly virtual office birthday celebration or hundreds of daily spam emails? Fight the new hire mental brainwashing. You can do it. Put on those hiking boots, grab that compass, turn on your out-of-office email notifications, and let's explore.

Here's three reasons why it's important to get out of the office periodically:

TO KEEP UP WITH YOUR EVOLVING PROFESSION

You've checked all the right learning boxes so far as you've gained knowledge about the company and your role, plus still have your academic knowledge in your back pocket. That's great, but your profession isn't going to stop moving and your position is going to evolve. You don't want the knowledge train to pass you by, which means engaging in pertinent professional development.

Ask your manager and colleagues to suggest appropriate professional development opportunities. If they aren't aware of any, ask your colleagues and the peers you've met at other companies. When you start researching options, you'll see that professional development comes in many shapes and sizes:

✔ Industry and role-specific webinars
✔ Industry conferences or association meetings (virtual and in person)
✔ Professional certification programs (virtual and in person)

Select the professional development opportunities that make the most sense based on the feedback received, your interests, and the expectations of your role.

YOU'LL ENHANCE YOUR RELATIONSHIPS WITH PEERS

As mentioned earlier in the book, it will benefit you and your company to meet as many peers in other companies as possible. With those whom you click with, get to know them even better to establish greater trust. While you'll want to stay within legal bounds of what you are allowed and not allowed to discuss, you'll find that you can share enough information to truly support each other in your roles. Plus, these peers will be a shoulder to lean on because they know exactly what you are going through. We all need that once in a while.

The best way to get to know your peers is through spending time together at in-person or virtual conference and association meetings. There's a good chance they will be attending the same events as you. You'll have a perfect opportunity to talk shop and mutual interests during your downtime.

When your manager learns that you've become closer with a peer in another company, it will elicit a big smile.

If it's a competitor, you may even get a medal in the form of "great job"—a win-win situation as you like the person you've connected with, and your manager sees it as a benefit to the company.

YOUR CONSULTANTS AND VENDORS HAVE A WEALTH OF HELPFUL KNOWLEDGE

Getting to know your consultants or vendors is similar to developing relationships with your peers. Think about it for a second. If they are working with you, they are probably working with similar clients. This means they are in a position to share best practices (aka what their other clients are doing successfully and unsuccessfully). That said, take your relationship with them to the next level because they will often be willing to share the wealth.

The easiest way to achieve this is making time to meet with your vendors and consultants to talk shop. Take these moments to discuss ways other companies have solved issues you are dealing with, or initiatives they may be working on. These initiatives may be of value to your company, too, and they'll be happy to discuss them (cough ... more money for them ... cough).

They may also be able to provide a response to the famous executive question, "What are other companies doing?" Additionally, if a vendor has a client advisory council (a group of their clients that meets on a periodic basis to share feedback and advise the vendor on strategic direction), see if you can participate virtually or in person so you will get to meet and network with a group of peers. You've almost escaped your workplace, just a few more steps.

Oh no! There are two guards blocking your exit: Mr. Value and Ms. Budget. Let's talk about how you can appease each of these picky people to make your escape complete.

Mr. Value just needs one thing to be satisfied—knowing that whatever you are doing benefits both you and the company. So before asking to attend a conference or accepting an invitation to participate on a client advisory council, put together a business case that demonstrates the value your participation will bring to you and your company. Focus on the value-add educational content and networking opportunities with peers in similar businesses. Present the business case to your manager. If your manager likes what they see, good chance Mr. Value will let you through.

Ms. Budget is a little pickier than her partner. She will be satisfied if she feels the value of attending outweighs the cost. The good news is Ms. Budget doesn't care about free opportunities assuming you've appeased Mr. Value. This often includes webinars and local association meetings.

For development opportunities with a cost, here's my recommendation to optimize your chances of satisfying Ms. Budget. First, see if any events are sponsored by consultants or vendors you currently do business with as sometimes they can provide free or discounted tickets. Just make sure you stay within your company's boundaries of accepting "gifts" from consultants and vendors. In addition, research professional development opportunities for the upcoming year before annual budgets are developed. Then make your business case to attend. Taking this approach will minimize pressure on your manager because they won't need to say no or look for money if you present a strong business case. They can add your event costs into the proposed annual budget.

Whenever you gain the opportunity to professionally develop yourself, make sure you put the cherry on top. What this means is, when you return to the office, put together a synopsis of what you learned that offers value to you and the company. Share it with your manager and colleagues. Not only will they gain an opportunity to better themselves through your shared knowledge, but you will also show that you attended for the right reasons (in other words, you didn't just attend the conference for the free food and drinks). Your manager, plus Mr. Value and Ms. Budget, will remember this when you ask to attend your next professional development opportunity.

Tales from the Inside

Taylor, an allocations manager at Coral 33, a clothing retailer, got a call from Dylan, her peer at Northern Outdoors, another clothing retailer, letting her know a new retail allocations association had just been formed. Dylan was on the association's board and was tasked with gaining membership for the group. Dylan invited Coral 33 to join the association at a cost of $3,000 per year.

Taylor was excited to become a member as her leadership team, up to the CEO, commonly asked how other companies handled allocating merchandise to their stores. Given she didn't know that many of her peers, it was often difficult to find the answer. However, Taylor knew that Dylan's timing was poor as the annual budget had just been approved for the next year.

Considering the circumstances, how should Taylor approach this situation?

Taylor could let Dylan know that Coral 33 was unable to join for the upcoming year because she didn't budget the $3,000 for the association membership. However, she knew she'd be doing a disservice to herself and Coral 33. So she took this approach instead:

Taylor called Dylan and said, "Can you please send me two sets of information—the benefits of becoming a member of the association and the names of companies that have joined?"

Upon receipt of the information, Taylor set up some time with her manager to make a business case for this opportunity. Taylor started by saying, "I know we didn't budget for it, but we have a tremendous opportunity to improve and enhance Coral 33's allocations processes for $3,000."

When her manager simply said, "Tell me more," Taylor did. She explained that Coral 33 had the opportunity to join a newly formed allocations association with the following benefits:

- ✔ Two membership meetings per year (in person and virtually); a list of the member names, titles, and contact information; and monthly webinars led by reputable speakers on allocations topics of interest to the company.
- ✔ She would be able to meet and develop relationships with her peers in allocations from other companies, including Wheat Mill Designs and Regato Fashions, two competitors.
- ✔ This would put her in the position to gain allocations knowledge from her peers, plus she'd be one email away from answering executive questions about other companies.
- ✔ The $3,000 annual membership fee is $2,000 less than the company paid to consultants last year to better understand the allocations approaches other clothing retailers were taking.
- ✔ By joining at the association's inception, she would have a great opportunity to get allocations topics of specific importance to Coral 33 on upcoming meeting agendas and webinars.

✓ She would gain the opportunity to develop and grow in her role given what she would learn from the meetings, webinars, and her peers.

Taylor then crossed her fingers, hoping she satisfied Mr. Value and Ms. Budget by demonstrating the significant pipeline of value-add knowledge the membership would introduce to her and Coral 33 at a fraction of the cost that the company had paid for such knowledge in the past. Taylor's manager told her that she not only convinced him to join but Coral 33 was actually going to save money. Another $5,000 had been allocated to consultant fees in the recently approved budget so the company would actually save $2,000 for the upcoming year. That said, Taylor was thrilled as she not only gained an excellent professional development opportunity but was applauded for her efforts in networking with her peers.

CHAPTER TWELVE

Your Workspace Showcase

I call this the money chapter. While I'd love to tell you how to make fifties and hundreds rain from the sky, unfortunately, my definition is not as dramatic. Hopefully, though, it will be more fulfilling than snatching Benjamins and Ulysseses from the air. Why? I focus on the importance of making your office or remote workspace the million-dollar place to visit.

Let's start with the obvious. It's never in your best interest to have a messy workspace. Sure, some may say this is a sign of genius, but in my experience, management and colleagues see it as a sign of a disorganized employee. If someone can't see the majority of your desk when they walk in or on camera, it's too messy. If someone sees yesterday's lunch on your desk, it's too dirty. If cleanliness and neatness just aren't possible for you, don't bother reading the rest of this chapter. Just hope you work in the one office in the universe where no one looks at your workspace, or someone has invented a hologram of a clean workspace you can use.

While having a clean and organized workspace is highly recommended, cleanliness alone does not satisfy the working smart test. You want your workspace to be unique and draw visitors in like a frogfish's wiggly lure (I digress as you don't want to eat them; you just want them to visit). Why? Because you can use your workspace to your competitive advantage. Just think, if you perfect the art of the unique workspace, you may become the host of a workspace-design reality show someday.

Think about the last grocery store you were in. You know there's a psychological strategy regarding the merchandise placement, right? Bright produce colors entice you to walk in, various kinds of merchandise dot your path toward the must-have dairy in the back, and impulse buys, like candy, gum, and magazines, tempt you at the register.

With this setup, including tidy shelves, the expectation is this design will maximize sales.

Now, pretend you're a grocery store manager but instead of selling food, you're selling an impression, and your workspace is your supermarket. The way you configure your office, cubicle, or remote workspace is how you maximize your value and grow. So let's start selling grow-ceries. Here's the blueprint for effectively marketing your workspace to your manager and colleagues:

✔ The lawyer in me feels compelled to lead with this. Make sure your office decorations are allowable per company policy. I've seen refrigerators, holiday lights, and heaters allowed in some and not in others. You don't want the ASPs or facilities police to come knocking. Also, you are at work to work. Yes, your office showcase can help you meet your colleagues, but don't make it the office hangout. Your manager will notice if you are spending your days talking to Emma, Kayla, Hunter, and Jared.

✔ Place unique items up front, doing your best to make them within eyeshot of anyone passing by or seeing them on camera. These can be objects you've collected while traveling, family mementos, or even seashells that look like US states. They are bound to pique employee curiosity and generate conversation: "Oh wow! A conch that looks like Texas!"

✔ Place pictures of family members, friends, pets, or unique experiences all around your workspace as everyone is curious (nosy) about pictures. This will keep them in your office or virtual workspace as they will create another communications opportunity: "You really met Billy Crystal at Applebee's?"

MAINTAIN THE OVERALL POSITIVE APPEARANCE OF YOUR WORKSPACE.

✔ As discussed earlier, keep your workspace neat and organized. This means ensuring your desktop is as clear as possible and placing any papers in neat piles. Maximize the use of electronic files. It gives you more space and gets you points for being green.

✔ Don't leave anything confidential on your desk. It's never a good habit, plus it's certainly not something you want to showcase on the tour of your workspace.

✔ Remember, it's not actually a grocery store. Put any food or drinks away before leaving at the end of the day. Even if they aren't empty, the simple appearance of them makes your area look sloppy. Plus, you don't want unnecessary visitors at night.

✔ Each time you eat in your workspace, wipe your desk down with antibacterial wipes. Not only will it address any messes or smells, but cleaning will leave a nice shine on your desk, which presents great optics.

✔ Add some plants that will thrive in your workspace and

keep them well maintained. They are pleasant to look at, plus will improve air quality by removing harmful pollutants. If you don't have kids, you can tell people these are your babies. Maybe even name them as that will certainly generate more conversation. Then again, maybe not.

BY TAKING THE GROCERY STORE APPROACH TO YOUR WORKSPACE

✓ You've opened the door (no pun intended if you have an office) for everyone to get to know you better as you've introduced many visuals leading to easy talking points: "You met Billy Crystal in an Applebee's while he was holding a conch that looked like Texas?" At a minimum, you'll have a good chat, and at a maximum, you'll be developing a relationship.

✓ You'll be more emotionally healthy. A messy, unorganized desk area is likely going to cause unnecessary stress, especially when you can't find what you need. Plus, the plants will help.

✓ You are going to be judged on your workspace's appearance. If it's unique, clean, and organized, you are going to be seen in a better light. If it's just another workspace, you won't gain or lose points. If it's a dumpster, your audience will have a hard time being convinced that your work performance isn't the same—unless your boss is Oscar the Grouch. It's critical you show the office that you have your stuff together and that you're an interesting person.

Here's the best news: taking the actions to be interesting and organized shouldn't take you more than ten minutes a day. Just water some plants, put your papers in a pile, and reposition your shell collection to create a map of the United States. The bottom line is that by being strategic and conscientious, you have an opportunity to positively market yourself to your entire office, without having to leave your workspace.

Tales from the Inside

The most interesting workplace sights I've seen are these:

✓ **Twenty-gallon fish tank:** As you can imagine, everyone in the office knew this employee. I would go so far as to say she was the poster child of working smart as some employees took such a liking to specific fish in her tank (even naming them!), they would find a reason to stop by her office often. While there, she would work many business deals to her advantage as whoever was in her office was talking to Rupert the catfish.

✓ **Ecosphere:** One of my colleagues had an ecosphere (a large sphere that contained tiny shrimp that fed on algae) on the front corner of his desk. Those passing by his workspace saw the sphere and looked inside out of curiosity. Seeing the little shrimp swimming around elicited feedback—everything from "That's so cool!" to "Why would you want that?" While he was labeled the shrimp man, he took it as a badge of honor as he was able to meet and converse with everyone in the office.

✓ **Cats:** A colleague working remotely had two cats that loved to make appearances on her camera. They definitely thought they were employees too. Sometimes they'd be on her shoulders, her keyboard, and the windowsill next to her workspace. The best was when they put their faces up against the camera out of curiosity. Fortunately, their curiosity did not kill them. They definitely brightened any meeting, and the cat lovers couldn't get enough of them.

✓ **Magic 8-Ball:** A woman who reported to me had a Magic 8-Ball on her desk. Given the fact that everyone wants their future predicted, it became a reason for many people to stop by, ask a question, shake it, and hope for the answer they were looking for. This created an opportunity for her to meet and get to know many employees. The ones who got the answer they wanted were especially nice.

✓ **Brick office:** I am not talking about the outside of the building. I am talking about an office inside the building. Yes, I said that right. A colleague laid red brick in front of the drywall in his office. As you can imagine, everyone walking by for the first time did a double-take, saying, "Did I just see a brick office?" and would turn around and enter the office for a closer look. This enabled him to meet everyone in the office, and even visitors who thought this was the most interesting effect they'd ever seen.

✓ **Mini forest:** If I've learned anything in twenty-five years, I've learned that people love plants in their office. Whether it's for stress relief or for cleaner air, everyone has their reasons. In one workplace, a colleague had so many plants in his office, it looked like a greenhouse. The visual alone was enough to draw people into his office and usually elicited comments like, "What kinds of plants are these?" "Do you have to water them a lot?" and "My plants always die." They truly did see the forest for the trees.

CHAPTER THIRTEEN

Working from Afar

"Mary, you are on mute."
"Felipe, are you still in North Carolina?"
"I need an ergonomic chair."

Welcome to the world of remote work where laptops and internet connections rule the day. Remote work (sometimes referred to as WFH, work from home) is not a new concept, but it's become more prevalent as a result of the COVID-19

pandemic. In early 2020, many companies had to shut their physical workplaces. To carry on business effectively, employees were transitioned to a remote work environment. Given demonstrated employee productivity and company cost savings in 2020, some companies decided to permanently move to a remote work model. I think we'll see more companies move that direction for their employees who can reasonably work remotely.

As a new employee, you may be asked to temporarily or permanently work remotely in your job. So instead of your welcoming party being held in the conference room, it will be over a virtual meeting, and instead of chatting with employees in the hall, you will be chatting with them over instant messaging.

It's naturally going to be more challenging to showcase who you are and what you're capable of as a new employee in a remote work setting as many colleagues don't know much about you and haven't seen you around the office. However, using the work smart tactics you've learned so far, coupled with additional opportunities outlined in this chapter and beyond, you'll make everyone think they truly know you.

Whether working from home or remotely (perhaps in a coffee shop to escape the distractions at home) is part of your job description or a short-term or temporary arrangement, working smart in a remote work environment takes effort. As such, focus on executing the following:

FOLLOW THE COMPANY'S REMOTE WORK POLICY RULES.
You'll likely have many reading materials as a new employee. Make sure this one is near the top of the pile because you'll be working remotely on day one, and the last thing you want to do is violate a remote work policy, especially with an audience of people who only know you through a computer screen.

ENSURE CONFIDENTIALITY.
While confidentiality is likely outlined and even bolded in your company's remote work policy, make sure to strictly abide by this rule. You don't want to have to call your new manager to let them know you accidentally left your laptop at the local bagel shop or wonder where the company's financial spreadsheets went that were on your home printer.

USE YOUR WORK-ISSUED COMPUTER FOR WORK.
You are going to have breaks, lunch, and maybe even some brief downtime during the workday. Minimize the use of your work-issued computer for personal interests during this time. Let's start with the simple premise that there's a good chance your company has access to see whatever you are doing on your computer. Constantly checking out your Instagram, playing games, or sending personal emails may seem like a nonissue to you but not to your company who will not only have security concerns about what sites you are visiting but how much work time you are spending on

personal interests. Don't get on your company's radar for this reason. Use your cell phone or personal computer for personal interests.

Also, don't download anything personal to your work computer. Sure, anything you download or upload may be completely innocent like pictures from your vacations or holidays, but remember two things: you are going to give the computer back someday and you may forget to remove whatever you've downloaded or uploaded, and if you download from internet sites, you run the risk of getting a virus on your work computer and then having to deal with potential policy violations, lost data, and being without your computer for a while. It's not worth it.

AGREE UPON A SCHEDULE WITH YOUR MANAGER.
Talk to your manager about their schedule and see how closely you can sync up with it. Given the information I've shared in previous chapters about spending time with your manager, you'll want to maximize the amount of time you are working at the same time, especially for the first few months.

BE RESPONSIBLE.
In addition to following the company remote work policy, make sure you don't give your manager a reason not to trust you in your remote environment. At a minimum, this means being available during your scheduled hours,

ensuring your work performance, including deliverables, meets their expectations, and avoiding temptations like watching Hulu.

MINIMIZE DISTRACTIONS.

Distractions are inevitable no matter where you work, whether it is at home, in a coffee shop, or in your car. However, distractions in a remote environment differ from those in an office environment. What comes to mind are children, siblings, parents, pets, coffee shop customers, and doorbells.

To the best of your ability, find a quiet location for the hours you are scheduled to work or take actions to make the environment quiet by wearing headphones. I know that's often easier said than done, but making the effort will be noticed and appreciated by your manager and colleagues as they will see a positive difference in your work productivity.

I knew a colleague who was responsible for watching his two-year-old daughter during work hours. For every thirty minutes he attended meetings, about fifteen of those minutes would be productive and the other fifteen would be the audience listening to him speak with his daughter. His manager had a constructive conversation with him about his poor work productivity, and he took two actions to improve the situation: his parents started watching his daughter during work hours a few days a week, and he changed his work hours to maximize his productivity on the days he was responsible for watching her.

DON'T WORK 24/7.

Employees will have different schedules in a remote work environment. So if you try to talk to Roxanne at 7:00 every morning (because she is an early riser) but also Jeremy at 7:00 every night (because he is a night owl), you will inevitably burn yourself out. Make sure to adhere to the schedule that you and your manager agreed upon and work with the resources available to you during those times. Sure, there will be days when you need to get up extra early or work extra late, but make them the exception, not the norm.

RESPECT EVERYONE'S WORK SCHEDULES.

You will have your schedule. Your manager and colleagues will have their schedules. You want everyone to respect your schedule so make sure you respect theirs. They don't want to work 24/7 either. Consider colleagues in different time zones because their schedules will have the time zone component to them too. Working in California, I know my New York colleagues don't want to hear from me at 5:00 p.m. my time (8:00 p.m. their time), and I don't want to hear from them at 5:00 a.m. my time (8:00 a.m. their time). First impressions mean everything, and this one is especially important.

BUILD RELATIONSHIPS.

As you've seen in the previous chapters, one of the cornerstones of working smart is ensuring you develop relationships throughout your workplace. This doesn't change in a remote environment, but it becomes more challenging as you won't be getting to know Christy at the water cooler and Wes in the breakroom. That said, I recommend showcasing yourself in as many situations as possible. This doesn't mean getting up and doing a song and dance nor interrupting your CFO during a virtual meeting; it means engaging whenever you have the appropriate opportunities. Whether that's making it a point to introduce yourself at the beginning of virtual meetings or putting a unique decoration behind you that is bound to generate interest and questions while on camera, your colleagues will have a chance to get to know and understand you.

LEARN AND UNDERSTAND YOUR MENTAL HEALTH BENEFITS.
Lack of in-person socialization may cause you to become lonely or depressed and negatively affect your work performance. Research and take advantage of the mental health benefits available to you (check your employee assistance program or medical insurance plan), which may include virtual or in-person psychologist or psychiatrist visits.

ASK FOR WHAT YOU NEED.
Sure, you're likely to have pens and paper in your remote work environment, but what about a printer and two computer monitors? You may not get everything you want, but it's fair to request the materials you need to effectively

perform your job. Often, your company will have a policy associated with the materials and a process to obtain them, so if you aren't familiar with it, ask human resources.

• • •

Okay, now that you've got the basics of this remote work thing down, let's talk virtual meetings. Remember all the emails I said you're going to get. Similarly, you're likely to be invited to many, many meetings in a remote environment. Let's talk virtual meeting etiquette.

Virtual Meeting Etiquette

One of the most important points when it comes to—
Ruff, ruff!

Sorry about that. Now, where was I? Oh yes. Make sure you always—
"DO YOU WANT ANYTHING AT THE STORE?"

As I was saying, it's crucial that you—
Chomp, chomp!

You might recognize these sounds as the joys of virtual meetings. Let's talk about ways you can work smart in your virtual meetings.

IF YOU SCHEDULE THE MEETING, DON'T SCHEDULE IT FOR A FULL HOUR OR HALF HOUR.

Meetings are more common in the remote world because there aren't any informal ways to get people together (in other words, you can't just grab Bob from his cube and walk into Susan's office to talk to her). As such, there's a good chance you are going to schedule or be invited to multiple meetings each day.

Given this dynamic, if you don't have breaks between meetings, you are never going to get to the restroom or eat a snack. So whenever you schedule a meeting, leave time before the next meeting would typically start (for example, schedule a one-hour meeting for fifty minutes and a thirty-minute meeting for twenty-five minutes). Remember bonus points from the earlier chapter. This will earn you major points with the attendees.

ACCLIMATE YOURSELF WITH THE VIRTUAL MEETING TECHNOLOGY BEFORE MEETINGS.

Whether it's signing in or testing the camera, chat feature, and mute button, it will be very distracting if you are trying to figure the features out for the first time when you are in the meeting. Plus, no one wants to hear, "Mom, where are the car keys?" when someone is presenting something important and you don't know where the mute button is. Testing the features ahead of time will make you look well prepared and avoid any embarrassing missteps.

BE ON TIME.

A virtual meeting is no different than an in-person meeting for which others are counting on you to be on time. While sometimes being late is inevitable, especially when other meetings run over, make it the exception, not the norm, especially because you can't use an excuse like bad traffic or a late bus. Plus, apologize for being late if the opportunity presents itself.

BE PRESENT AND INTERESTED.

As a new employee, meetings are going to introduce an opportunity to demonstrate you are listening, learning, and engaging in the subject matter. Sure, it will be more difficult to engage when you first start as the discussion may sound like everyone is speaking another language, but ask questions to show you are present and interested. In time, you'll start to understand their language and engage more in the conversation, showing everyone what you are capable of.

MINIMIZE DISTRACTIONS AROUND YOU.

Put yourself in a room with no visual or audible distractions, just as if you were in a meeting room. That's easier said than done, I know, so here is my recommendation: for any distractions within your control, do what it takes to minimize them. Otherwise, such distractions could annoy attendees and throw the meeting off course.

I don't want to pick on spouses, kids, and pets, but they are usually the distractions within your control (I am married, and have three kids and a dog, so I know it's not that easy.). Work with them on proper spacing in the house where you can't hear them and they can't hear you. That may be the garage or attic, but so be it. Plus, you may distract your audience if you constantly turn the camera on and off, walk around the house with your camera on, or talk to the person on your left or your right (even if you are on mute). Also, wear headphones with a microphone to minimize any noise heard around you.

For distractions out of your control, like the doorbell or your baby waking up from a nap, do the best you can to minimize the impact when these events occur. Your attendees will be rooting for you, as they have all been there too.

MASTER THE ART OF MUTE.
Using mute effectively is an art. Why? You are going to need to know when to turn the sound on to make yourself heard but then turn the sound off to avoid everyone hearing what's going on in your world. Perfecting the art of jockeying the mute button back and forth to your and your audience's satisfaction is an absolute must. Speaking of mute, turn ringers off on your smartphone and house phone (if you have one) as they are distracting.

MINIMIZE MULTITASKING.

It's so tempting to multitask during the meeting. Why? Because you likely have a lot of work on your plate and are confident you can get away with shredding a stack of financials or responding to your emails while listening. Here's my recommendation if you are on camera: if you can naturally do two things at once (pay attention to the meeting and perform other work), go for it. Just make sure you disguise what you are doing in a way where you aren't causing a distraction (minimize your eye shifting). However, if you are multitask challenged (can't do two things at once), need to pay close attention to this particular meeting, or could get called on at any minute, do not multitask. There's nothing worse than getting called on in a meeting where you haven't paid an ounce of attention. The red of your face will light up like a Christmas ornament for all to see. Instead, talk to your manager about your heavy workload and land on a different way to get it accomplished.

AVOID EATING.

Food is inherently distracting, whether it's what you are eating or how you are eating it. Annoying, right? I can assure you, you are not going to starve, so wait on the food. It's not worth taking a character hit over a ham sandwich and Coke.

DRESS APPROPRIATELY.

If you are on camera, dress appropriately for your respective audience. Why? Because not only do you want to uphold the professionalism of yourself and your company, but you don't want to distract your audience with Pokémon T-shirts with ketchup stains, tuxedos, or ballgowns.

BE COGNIZANT OF YOUR FACIAL EXPRESSIONS.

Be aware of the faces you make on camera, as everyone can see your looks of happiness, disgust, or confusion. I'm not saying you need to have a poker face or big smile throughout the whole meeting, but just be aware that your expressions are being seen and analyzed as your audience is just seeing your face.

USE AN APPROPRIATE BACKGROUND.

Just like we talked about making sure your workspace is clean and tidy, ensure your remote background looks the same. Think simple, tasteful art or blank backgrounds versus dirty kitchens or political signs with controversial slogans. If you use the electronic backgrounds, rethink if you really want to be in the International Space Station or amusement park ride. Something office-like would be professional and appropriate.

These all sound like basic virtual meeting ground rules—because they are. So how does this support working smart? Most employees will only follow some of these rules. If you follow all of them, those who invite you to virtual meetings will do so with a smile on their face, rather than think to themselves, "Oh no, what am I going to see or hear?"

Starting the first day of your new job in shorts may seem weird, but it's one of the benefits of working remotely. You'll also enjoy eating at home, no commute, and being able to answer the door for your package deliveries. That said, demonstrate your respect for this opportunity by making sure you follow the company remote work rules and showcasing your value to your manager and colleagues. Give them the impression you are sitting right outside their door.

Tales from the Inside

Jordan was hired as a sales representative at Duster's Automotive. When he was offered the position, his manager, Rachel, said he could work from home. Jordan was thrilled as his commute would have been over an hour each way. This is what Jordan's first three months at Duster's Automotive looked like:

- ✔ Jordan met all his sales goals.
- ✔ Jordan was great on the phone with customers.
- ✔ Jordan was technology challenged. He knew how to write emails but not much more than that.

✔ Jordan was a night owl and liked to stay up late to work.

✔ Jordan lives with a roommate who has a cat and two dogs.

After three months, Rachel met with Jordan in a virtual meeting to share his ninety-day review. What do you think she talked about?

✔ She applauded him for meeting his sales goals.

✔ She praised his positive customer service approach because she'd received feedback that he consistently gave his customers peace of mind they were buying quality products at a fair price.

✔ She recommended he talk to the IT department to learn how to use the company's virtual meeting technology effectively. He had been late for meetings (he never knows the right buttons to push to get in) and didn't manage the mute button effectively (as meeting attendees were often distracted by his roommate and pets).

✔ Knowing that Jordan sends emails late at night (as she's been the recipient of many), she reminded him of the company's policy that emails should only be sent during the core business hours of 8:00 a.m. to 5:00 p.m. In fact, Jordan's colleague, Lisa, expressed concern with getting urgent emails from Jordan at 10:30 p.m. after working long days. Rachel recommended he work with IT to schedule emails he drafts late at night to be automatically sent in the morning.

✔ She told Jordan the food wrappers and his disheveled appearance in morning virtual meeting backgrounds conveyed an unprofessional look to his audience, which sometimes included customers, and said he needed to keep himself and his workspace clean.

Rachel concluded the meeting by letting Jordan know the company was satisfied with his sales performance but his remote work habits needed to improve.

CHAPTER FOURTEEN

Smorgasbord of Working Smart

I've always wanted to use the word *smorgasbord*, so I'm using this book as my chance. Welcome to your smorgasbord of working smart opportunities (also known as information that's important enough to be in the book but not substantive enough to warrant an entire chapter):

Demonstrate

I have the word *demonstrate* permanently etched in my brain. Why? Consistently throughout my career, I was taught that decision-makers expect you to *demonstrate* need and value (remember Mr. Value and Ms. Budget from an earlier chapter) for basically anything requested.

As such, over twenty-five years, I've focused on demonstrating the need and value for everything from a stapler to attending a high-priced conference. I've seen the greatest success using data to demonstrate. Simply asking for something and expecting you'll get it, like you did with your parents for the lollipop at the barber shop, won't cut it anymore. Save the kicking and screaming and tears because those won't work either.

For example, you may see others in the office with faster computers. Simply asking for a new computer because Destiny in accounting has a better one will likely fail. Instead, use data to demonstrate your need for a faster computer. Data points could include showing the following:

- ✔ The last time you got a new computer
- ✔ That you can't satisfy your colleagues who count on timely information because your computer isn't fast enough
- ✔ How it will allow you to get work done faster

Before you think I've just given you the silver bullet to gain everything you desire in the workplace, unfortunately

I haven't. Often times, lack of budget, cultural differences, or competing priorities will result in denials. However, don't let that stop you as making sure you demonstrate will be seen as professional and always presents a better chance of prevailing.

Be Open to and Learn from Constructive Feedback

As hard as you focus on working smart in your new job, you are going to experience missteps. Everyone does. Believe it or not, you'll actually work smarter by accepting feedback, including performance improvement recommendations, from those you trust. Why? Because—

✔ You'll demonstrate maturity as you are open to and capable of receiving constructive feedback.

✔ You'll create an opportunity to show growth in your role if you accept and apply feedback.

✔ It's likely you'll learn something about the company you can now apply to future situations.

Let me give you an example. Todd (in human resources) learned from the insurance carrier that Anna, an executive, needed to provide additional information in order for her supplemental life insurance policy to be approved. Todd sent Anna an email asking her to provide the required information to the insurance carrier. Within ten minutes,

Todd's phone rang. It was Jose, his manager, who said, "I just got a call from Anna wondering why she received the email you sent her."

Perplexed, Todd said, "I sent it because Anna was on the list of employees who needed to provide additional information to the insurance carrier to be approved for supplemental life insurance."

Jose then said, "You're right, but you shouldn't have sent the email to Anna as she and the other executives prefer us to handhold them through anything benefits-related. Don't you remember this as we discussed it during your first week?"

Todd said, "I'm sorry. I forgot. I was on information overload during my first week. Is there anything I can do to fix the situation?"

"No, I handled it. Let's just be more cognizant of this in the future," Jose said.

Todd hung up and put Anna on speed dial as he wanted to be sure he remembered to treat her like a VIP for any future benefit issues.

Be the Bigger Person

As much as you think everyone plays by the rules in the office, many don't. No need to sugarcoat it, because you need to be prepared for it.

When I say people don't play by the rules, I am not talking about breaking the law. I am referring to being unfair, lazy, or rude. The frustrating part is that, often, these employees have relationships with senior leaders who tolerate such behavior. Go figure.

Here's an example. Leah started working at Hayden Imports as a compensation manager. Shortly after starting, she learned she was responsible for comanaging Elizabeth, an analyst who split her time equally between compensation and recruiting. One day, Leah learned that Elizabeth was leaving the organization because her mother was ill. Leah met with Corri, Elizabeth's recruiting comanager, and they agreed that whoever they found to replace Elizabeth would play the same role. After this meeting, Corri went alone to make a business case to Frank, her manager, to hire Elizabeth's replacement as her own full-time employee. Corri happened to be close to Frank as she had reported to him for twelve years. Frank approved it. Corri never gave Leah a good explanation why she went behind her back. As you can imagine, Leah had a hard time trusting Corri from that day forward. Fortunately, Leah's manager, Samantha, supported Leah by gaining approval for a half-time headcount to replace Elizabeth.

That said, minimize your time with the Corris of the workplace. When you must work with them, try to gain a commitment from your manager or mentor to help you deal with their shortcomings so your work product isn't negatively impacted.

If their behavior affects you personally, use the benefits of your employee assistance program to talk to a therapist.

The good news is there will always be someone to provide advice and guidance that you may have never thought of on your own when knee-deep in tough moments.

Avoid Drama

Turn on the TV and flip through the channels. Odds are you are going to see some dramas. Similar to TV, drama exists in the workplace in the form of gossip, rumors, and overexaggerations.

Here's the deal when it comes to work drama. You are going to see and hear things you don't need to do your day job. Let's dive into the two parts of that sentence. The first part: "You are going to see and hear things ..." Given human nature, it's going to be difficult to look away from any drama that occurs, whether it's a no-holds-barred argument, wild rumor, or excited rant.

Now the second part: "You don't need to do your day job." Based on my years of experience, I know that you don't need to get involved in drama to effectively perform your job. Trust me. I've seen employees get involved in drama due to the excitement of the moment to their detriment in the long run. Why? Because drama itself is not work-related, and good leadership doesn't have the time for it. That said, although tempting, I recommend you keep your drama to the TV set.

Drama came to Evelyn in the form of a standoff between two departments. Evelyn was hired into a logistics manager role at Faithful Trucking. As she met her new colleagues during her first week, she quickly learned that the logistics and finance departments did not care for each other. One day, Joselyn, the finance manager, asked Evelyn to meet with her. Joselyn had met Evelyn a few days earlier, and they hit it off over their love of snowboarding.

After some small talk, Joselyn started asking Evelyn very pointed questions about the logistics team, including inquiring about the personalities of different team members. Evelyn felt uncomfortable with Joselyn's questions. Fortunately for Evelyn, she wasn't able to answer any as she had only been with Faithful Trucking for two weeks. Over the next few weeks, Evelyn did her best to avoid Joselyn because she had no interest in getting involved in department drama.

MacGyver Approach

For those of you not familiar with MacGyver, it was a TV show in which the titular character improvised a solution to get out of a tricky situation with whatever items he could find. As such, going MacGyver is the ultimate form of working smart. If you become MacGyver in your office, you are effectively proving you can make something happen that everyone would not have thought possible.

Here's what generally happens. After demonstrating your idea's need and value, including gaining leadership approval, it's ultimately denied due to lack of funds. So what's your next move? MacGyver it. Put on your thinking cap, get creative, talk to the resources around you, and ask your vendors to help. I hate to say it, but you are likely going to have to MacGyver more things than not. However, when you finish your MacGyvering (and according to my spell check, that *is* actually a word), the reaction from leadership will be priceless. They will be shocked what you just demonstrated for them could actually happen.

In one job, my team developed a comprehensive well-being program that met all the requirements leadership was looking for, except one—we didn't have the money to pay for the vendor-based program. Knowing the value of making employees aware of and understanding the importance of workplace well-being, we went back to the drawing board, put on our MacGyver hats, and tasked ourselves with building a well-being program with no budget.

Knowing our employee health data showed a high incidence of cancer and diabetes, we decided to offer free well-being "lunch and learns" to all employees on topics like the importance of eating well, diabetes prevention, smoking cessation, and managing diabetes. We set up the meetings in conference rooms that had long tables for employees to eat their lunch, invited reputable well-being speakers from our health insurance plan vendors, and offered healthy snacks (provided by the vendors).

We received positive feedback from the attendees. We heard, "We really appreciate you offering these topics,"

"We'd love to learn about financial well-being too," and "Thanks for the snacks." As we continued to offer the free "lunch and learns" on different well-being topics, we started to see greater enrollment and engagement in the different company benefits we spoke about and a reduction in the incidence of significant employee health issues. This resulted in a win for the employees, the benefits department, and the company. We successfully MacGyvered it.

Be a Utility Player

Look at your job description. I bet a line item in it says, "Other duties as assigned," or what I playfully refer to as utility player responsibilities. You know what that means, right? It means you will likely be asked to do tasks you don't typically do in your day job—within legal and ethical bounds, of course.

Here's some advice: if you are asked to do something you aren't familiar with, do not frown, complain, or run. Instead, scream, "Yes!" as loud as you can. Why? It's simple. If you are being asked to do something in this space, it means someone is in a bind and really needs your help. Think about it. Helping someone in a dire situation will make you feel good about yourself. Plus, the employee you support will likely let their leader know what a big help you were. It will be a big win because everyone remembers moments like this. In fact, it's a working smart win that truly stands above all others.

I've most commonly seen "other duties as assigned" in the form of manual labor, meaning someone is hosting a major meeting or a celebration and many hands are needed to carry food in, assemble tables and chairs, and clean up.

Communications in the Corner

Let's role-play. Imagine you are in a meeting to discuss a newly approved project and your name is "Communications." During the meeting, you raise your hand not once, not twice, but three times, as you know the project will need a communication component. However, no one calls on you. You hate to do it, but eventually you interrupt.

"This project sounds great," you proclaim, "but the deliverable won't be effective if it's collecting dust on our desks because no one knows about it."

There's a lot to unpack here. Let's start with the reason why no one called on you. No one called on you because talking about the project itself is much more exciting than talking about how to effectively communicate it. Next, let's address the dust on everyone's desks. If no one dedicates time to developing an effective communication plan, the project deliverable will just sit on everyone's desks, which isn't good for the employees who will benefit from it. I wish I were overexaggerating, but unfortunately, I've seen this occur nine times out of ten when discussing projects. Hopefully this won't happen to you, but here's what to do if it does.

Grab the communication reins and roll out your amazing project to its intended audience. Here are the keys to effective communication:

✔ **Make your intended audience aware.** It's critical to use communication channels that effectively reach your employees. For example, if your employees don't regularly use the computer, don't use email as your communication vehicle. If your employees speak different languages, make sure your communication is translated into the respective languages that employees speak.

✔ **Ensure your audience understands what you've made them aware of.** Once employees become aware, introduce appropriate education opportunities for them to learn what you're attempting to convey to them because understanding its value to them is critical.

If you achieve employee awareness and understanding, your audience will feel much more comfortable engaging—and that's a great feeling.

If you have the bandwidth to roll out an awareness and understanding communication plan yourself, fine. Just know that in many cases, resources like vendors or consultants associated with the project will gladly take the lead or lend support. Additionally, if you have an internal communication resource, they are often positioned to assist. Use them to the extent you can, as they are the experts.

Here's an example of how Sofia had to remind leadership that one-size-fits-all communications just doesn't work. Sofia was the benefits manager for Rancho Properties, a real estate development company. In the past year, the company acquired three hotels and seven apartment complexes, which meant 7,100 new service employees.

When Sofia started preparing for annual benefits open enrollment, she developed a chart showing how the benefits team planned on communicating the new benefits information to employees at every location. When she handed the chart to her manager, Liam, he said, "Aren't we just going to email the information to everyone?"

Sofia responded, "We could, but given the majority of our new employees don't have computers and speak multiple languages, many won't receive and understand the benefit materials."

Fortunately, Liam took a good hard look at the chart Sofia developed, which included email, mail, in-person, and multi-language communications, and they both focused on what needed to be done to successfully communicate the company's benefits to all employees.

Socialize

Why should attending holiday parties and other social events always be on your to-do list? Because of free food. No. Well, yes. But there's something even more important. These events present a low-key opportunity to meet and become memorable to employees you haven't met yet. So instead of taking the easy route and huddling with your security blanket (aka your inner circle), introduce yourself to everyone from senior leaders to fellow analysts and spend time getting to know them. Don't be nervous or intimidated. They are human, too, and there's a good chance you'll connect on a particular topic of interest.

If you want to take your memorable self to the next level, sing karaoke or even participate in the office skit. Colleagues will love it and certainly remember you. Presenting your human side introduces a reason for them to become interested in you and understand the overall value you bring. Plus, there's a good chance you've made them laugh and smile along the way.

One night I attended a work dinner at a nice steak restaurant with the human resources department. Some senior department leaders I hadn't met sat at my table. I saw this as a timely opportunity to get to know them. We initially engaged in some friendly conversation about sports and families, and the evening was going well.

When it came time to order, the waiter told me that a Caesar salad came with my meal. As I don't like Caesar dressing, I asked if I could have a vinaigrette instead. I didn't think anything of it as I had made that request plenty of times before with my family. Right after ordering, I looked to my left and my right and saw two senior leaders bust out laughing—at me.

In between cackles, they asked, "Did you just order vinaigrette dressing on a Caesar salad?"

My face turned red and I wanted to climb under the table. I even tried to call the waiter back and say, "I don't need the salad." But it was too late. When the salad arrived, the chorus of laughter started up again. Once I pulled myself together, I realized it was all in good fun.

Walking away from the dinner, I realized that I had not only met and developed relationships with two senior leaders but I am proud (and fortunate, after that event) to call them friends. In fact, whenever they email me, they call me Vinny Grette.

Be Open to Change

Only two things are certain in life—death and taxes. Well, I'm going to add a third—change. There is a 100 percent chance that workplace change is going to happen, and it will impact you. Knowing this, the key to success is how to appropriately react and respond to such change.

It's hard to predict reaction to change because everyone acts differently in the moment, especially to negative change. However, keep it professional. I know, easier said than done, but try really hard. It's important that your manager sees you react to it maturely.

Your response to change is where you have a real opportunity to show you know how to work smart. Fortunately (or unfortunately), I've had a lot of experience in this area, especially in the company where I had four different managers in five years. While it was frustrating having to start over with every new manager, I learned the importance of being mature in my response to each manager change. I knew that each new manager would want to get to know me and the value I brought to the company.

So, in addition to focusing on demonstrating my value personally, I encouraged each manager to talk to my inner circle. This not only gave me the confidence that my new manager would be influenced to some extent by what they heard from my coworkers but mitigated the impact of the change on me, as I felt good about what my circle would say.

Therefore, whenever you experience change and get over your reaction, think methodically about a response that will work to your and the company's advantage. Change could be the company is being sold. Your division is moving to New Jersey. A product is being discontinued. The company has acquired another company. Good change. Bad change. Focus on becoming very good at considering your response to change. Why? Because change is going to happen.

Face Your Fears

To succeed in the working world, it's important to be well-rounded. So get it over with sooner rather than later. What am I talking about?

Be willing and able to do professional things in the working world you are uncomfortable doing. I've seen many employees fall down when they've been put on the spot, and it's always painful to watch. Fears could be anything from standing up and making a presentation at your department meeting to having to fire someone to being asked to interview and hire a new employee. Get over and ahead of it. Talk to your manager about areas you'd like to improve. A good manager will gladly help and support you with professional development so that when your moment comes, you will be mentally prepared and ready.

One week after starting in a job, I was told that I'd be leading the two-hour benefits orientation for thirty new hires every two weeks. I almost quit on the spot. Being told this reminded me of the day I vomited in my driveway when I was on my way to my first violin concert. (True story. I never played the violin again after that concert.) I was absolutely terrified.

Fortunately, I wasn't thrown directly out of the human resources nest. The employee handing the training over to me adequately prepped me as I performed two dry runs with no one in the room, and one actual orientation session with her present. Fortunately, I held myself together as I walked into a live audience for the first time.

From that day for the next two years, I performed the orientation, and each time I found another opportunity to improve. Looking back, facing my fear at the time was incredibly scary, but the experience to overcome my fear of speaking to groups was one of the best outcomes to happen as now I feel comfortable presenting to audiences with over 1,000 people.

Request a "No Surprises" Pact with Your Manager

Shortly after starting, request a "no surprises" pact with your manager. Let them know you'd like immediate feedback—good, bad, and ugly (well, hopefully no ugly)—and can handle it. I know that sounds like commonsense, but unfortunately, many managers are conflict averse when it comes to providing constructive feedback on the spot. They take the less confrontational route by documenting such feedback in employee performance reviews where employees learn about it for the first time. This is unfair to the employee, because if they had known about their manager's concern, they would have had ample time to correct it before the performance review was written, and likely could turn negative feedback into a positive result. Plus, it often results in time inefficiencies as managers must address multiple "help me understand" questions from the employee, including why they waited until the performance review to bring awareness to the concern.

Gaining such feedback on the spot will also promote transparency, which is critically important in developing and maintaining a positive manager/employee relationship.

Put Your Cell Phone Aside

Your phone is going to buzz and ring all day. You know it and so do I. I am not going to tell you to ignore it every time that happens as there could be a legitimate emergency, but I'm going to tell you it's not in your best interest to have your cell phone glued to your hand all day. The simple optics of your cell phone in hand are going to give the perception you are spending more of your workday focusing on personal interests than work tasks. That said, be smart about when you pick up your cell phone. A few times a day and breaks/lunch would likely be deemed reasonable.

Work Romance, Written and Unwritten Rules

You may meet the love of your life at work. Simple, right? Date, fall in love, get married, enjoy life. Not so much. Think complex, as there are likely company rules around work romances, plus unwritten rules you'll want to seriously consider.

First, there's a good chance company policy will not allow you to date your manager. If there isn't a policy, I wouldn't recommend it anyway, and it would take another book to tell you all the reasons why. If you are going to date a colleague, check your company policy first. At a minimum, it's likely you will need to make human resources aware. If it's allowable, think about the risks associated with dating a colleague.

For one, some business situations could negatively impact your personal relationship (such as disagreements on business decisions, competing for prime projects and initiatives). Plus, between work and home, you may find yourself spending too much time with each other. Also, consider the impact if you break up, especially if you work closely together. Not only will situations become awkward (think meetings, projects, company events, and happy hours), but your performance may suffer given the inevitable distractions you will now be dealing with. Because you are new and proving yourself, the risk may not be worth it.

"Fantastic Five"

If you asked your colleagues to write character traits that have been advantageous in their careers (whether they helped them fit in or climb the career ladder) on a whiteboard, it's likely these five traits will be at the top of the list: consistent, trusted, fair, empathetic, and resilient. What makes this a great combination is the mix between business and emotional traits.

Focusing on making these traits the bedrock of your personality will put you at another advantage in the workplace (and life too) given the respect you will garner from your leadership and colleagues. I'll leave it to you to learn how to master these traits from the experts (think professional development and mentor from earlier in the book).

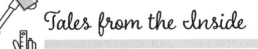

Tales from the Inside

Introducing my best attempt at a ditty about working smart (smorgasbord style):

Be on time...Hide the cell...

Meet the ASPs...Perform well...

Know the tech...Take care of you...

Admit mistakes...Learn what to do...

Face your fears...Lose the books...

Meet your peers...Perfect your look...

Make sure to smile...Balance you...

Avoid negativity...Learn something new...

Be consistent...Choose your crew...

No lip service...Develop you...

Get quick wins...Proofread all...

Minimize drama...Engage on calls...

Avoid love...Be fair...

Call a historian... Show you care...

Meet a mentor... Praise support...

Pay it forward...Ball's in your court...

Be social media smart...Resilient too...

Make a mark...You know what to do...

CHAPTER FIFTEEN

Saved the Best for Last

One more test then you're dismissed. What's the best part about working smart?

If you answered, "I have the ability to reap the benefits of making good judgments beyond what's typically expected of me in the work environment," or something to that effect, then you've made the most of this book, but it's not the answer I'm looking for. You didn't think I was done sharing all my secrets, did you? I've actually saved the best for last.

The best reasons to work smart are these:

✔ You can witness your audience's big smiles, jaws dropped, and shaking head moments when you demonstrate your unexpected good judgment. Every time you experience it, an indescribable feeling of empowerment, pride, intelligence, satisfaction, and excitement will come over you. It's a feeling you'll want to experience again and again because it never gets old.

✔ You will become more indispensable to the company. Job security is not certain in the working world, but knowing you've taken steps as a new employee to firmly establish yourself among those deemed necessary to the company is a major feat.

Before we wrap, I've got one request—pay it forward. After your first day, you aren't going to be new anymore, but everyone who walks in the door after you will be. As you go through your career, you're going to meet new hires. Take the time to make them feel comfortable and share your secrets of working smart. You'll have a treasure trove of examples—some you've learned in this book and others you've learned on your own.

Remember those smiles you generated every time you worked smart; you'll see the same smile on the new employee's face you just shared your advice and guidance with. Plus, if they use such information, not only will they benefit but you will too as they'll be performing like someone who's been with the company for five years versus seven months.

You are ready and are going to do great. Bust through the doors of your first job with this game plan in hand, including those memorable thank-you notes, company benefits guides, and fruitcakes (well, maybe not fruitcakes), and go those places you'll go!

Tales from the Inside

I appreciate your making it this far in the book. Now tell me how you should handle work emails. Just kidding. I know there's a lot to absorb and remember, so to summarize, I've created an abbreviated version of the working smart examples presented in this book. I encourage you to visit my website at www.edbraywrites.com where you can print a copy of this chart and post it at your workspace. By taking this approach versus having to periodically reference the book, you'll avoid the inevitable papercut—my last piece of working smart advice.

INVEST THE TIME TO LEARN YOUR COMPANY INSIDE AND OUT.

Key resources include your manager, colleagues, independent research, company historians, vendors, and consultants (as applicable).

CHAPTER 3 – LEAVE YOUR SCHOOLBOOKS AT THE DOOR

MAKE TIME FOR YOURSELF.

No matter how smart you work, there will always be more work. Demonstrate you know how to work smart and then leave the work for later. Go to the park, the gym, your family's house, or Walt Disney World.

CHAPTER 2 – BALANCE YOUR WORK/LIFE SEESAW

GET TO KNOW EVERY ADMINISTRATIVE SUPPORT PROFESSIONAL IN YOUR DEPARTMENT.

Show them the respect and appreciation they deserve and great things will happen for you.

CHAPTER 4 – GET TO KNOW THE ASPS
(AKA WORKPLACE SUPERHEROES)

FOCUS ON SATISFYING YOUR MANAGER'S OBJECTIVES BUT BE TRUE TO THE UNIQUE VALUE YOU BRING TO YOUR ROLE.

Demonstrate your interest and ability in satisfying what you know to be most important to your manager. Take initiative to give time back to your manager. Showcase the unique value of you.

CHAPTER 5 – BECOME MANAGER SMART

DEMONSTRATE YOUR INITIAL VALUE TO THE COMPANY.

Request high-importance, high-impact work you're capable of completing. This will likely include work that no one has been interested in assuming in the past.

CHAPTER 6 – GAIN QUICK WINS

DEMONSTRATE YOUR RESPECT AND COMMITMENT TO THE COMPANY.

Examples include meeting your industry peers, volunteering to support meetings, connecting with a mentor, and exhibiting memorable praise and gratitude.

CHAPTER 7 – EARN BONUS POINTS

BE CONSCIENTIOUS AS CARELESS MISTAKES CAN CARRY GREAT CONSEQUENCES.

Examples include ensuring you proofread your documents and not missing deadlines.

CHAPTER 8 – YOUR WORKING SMART TOOLBOX

BE TECHNOLOGY SMART.

For example, avoid posting anything that will get you or the company in trouble, send user-friendly emails, and cheerlead for the company on social media.

CHAPTER 8 – YOUR WORKING SMART TOOLBOX

PUT YOURSELF IN THE POSITION TO BE PHYSICALLY, FINANCIALLY, AND EMOTIONALLY HEALTHY.

Research and enroll in benefits that will support your overall health as this will put you in an optimal position to maximize your work performance.

CHAPTER 9 – BENEFIT YOU

**YOU CAN NEVER KNOW TOO MANY
OF THE RIGHT PEOPLE AT WORK.**

Make it a point to meet and surround yourself with a trusted and reliable group of individuals. They will make your job easier, so make sure you do the same for them.

CHAPTER 10 – ESTABLISH YOUR INNER CIRCLE

PROFESSIONALLY DEVELOP YOURSELF.

Find the time to professionally develop yourself, whether it be through attending webinars and conferences or gaining professional certifications. Demonstrate the value to your company by sharing the knowledge you've learned with management and colleagues.

CHAPTER 11 – DEVELOP YOURSELF (AND YOUR COMPANY)

**SHOWCASE THE UNIQUE VALUE OF YOUR
OFFICE OR REMOTE WORK SETTING.**

Design your workspace to attract those walking by or seeing it on camera as it will create an additional opportunity to meet everyone in the office.

CHAPTER 12 – YOUR WORKSPACE SHOWCASE

PERFECT THE SCIENCE OF WORKING FROM HOME.

Don't give anyone a reason to think you are incapable of working from home. In fact, take actions to demonstrate to your colleagues you are a remote work veteran in everything from your daily availability to being a virtual meeting pro.

CHAPTER 13 – WORKING FROM AFAR

**SHOW YOUR MANAGER AND COLLEAGUES
YOU ARE WISE BEYOND YOUR YEARS.**

For example, demonstrate, listen, be open to constructive feedback and change, be the bigger person, avoid drama, make the impossible possible, be a utility player, champion communications, request immediate manager feedback, be social, face your fears, be smart about your cell phone and work romances, and be consistent, trusted, fair, empathetic, and resilient.

CHAPTER 14 – SMORGASBORD OF WORKING SMART

PAY IT FORWARD.

Educate new employees about the working smart opportunities you've learned, plus any new working smart opportunities that you've become aware of.

CHAPTER 15 – SAVED THE BEST FOR LAST

Acknowledgments

Thank you to my readers. My hope is that the twenty-five years I put into this book translates to an amazing start to your career. Enjoy the ride!

Thank you to my wife, Christy, who has been by my side for twenty-seven years. This book would not have been possible without your patience, love, support, and cross-eyed looks as I pitched some of the craziest ideas to you. I can't smile without you. Let's never burn the day.

Thank you to my home team, Sarah, Corinne, and Liam. While living in Virginia, California, and Hawaii has allowed us to experience our own Disney *Up* adventure, I know it's come with much uprooting and sacrifice. I love you all and can't wait to watch you live out your own dreams.

Thank you to my mom, Betty-Jane, my brother, Scott, and my late dad, EJB Jr. You answered my million questions over the first twenty-two years of my life, which gave me the confidence to continue asking them once I got into the working world. I appreciate your love, generosity, and support.

Thank you to the seventeen managers I've reported to. I've learned something valuable from each of you. Special thanks to Kris Allison, Melanie Graper, Colleen Hudson, Jan Johnson, Nikki Jones-Gyllstrom, Craig Lock, Keri Lopez, Ed Page, Kevin Reimann, and Leny Riebli. Thank you to all of my mentors. I didn't know what the working world ropes looked like until you showed me. Special thanks to Wes Harper, Todd Lehman, Arte Nathan, Deon Riley, Evelyn Russell, Mark Stelzner, and Monte Young.

Thank you to everyone who has provided support and guidance in my career. Rolling down the business road is sometimes flat but often bumpy. Special thanks to those who helped me through the bumpy stretches, including Julie Anna Barker, Jennifer Benz, Annie Boneta, Susan Cotton, Elizabeth Garrett, Paul Hartman, Keith Hanleigh, Gayle Jenson, Ronda Magee, Marilyn Monahan, Jim Mulios, Dr. John Page, Lenny Pangesa, Ken Presant, Magan Ray, John Shelnutt, Michael Treichler, and Chris Tuininga.

Thank you to my good friends. We all need to blow off steam and who better to do it with than all of you. Special thanks to my Yorktown, NY, and Providence College crews.

Thank you to those who helped me turn the dream of writing a book into reality. Writing a book isn't easy. Your patience and guidance made it possible. Special thanks to my editor extraordinaire who worked me harder than I ever did in school, Sandra Wendel; my graphic designer who continuously kept it real, Domini Dragoone; my cover illustrator who brought my vision to life, Jess Estrella; my website designer, Logan Drake; my marketing specialists, Emily Fleming and Jason Neubauer; and the voices who added punch to my dialogue, Seth Miller, Kiley Raica, and Gabbie Meis.

To everyone I just mentioned, you've not only positively impacted me, but everyone who reads this book. You taught me how to work smart, and I'm excited to impart that knowledge to everyone starting their first job.

About the Author

Ed Bray grew up in a household where he started learning the art of working smart in the workplace through conversations with his father and grandfather, human resources executives at IBM for over seventy-five years combined.

When Ed was kicked out of the nest, he spent the next twenty-five years (and counting) working in human resources at ten companies, including Ross Stores, Inc., Hawaiian Airlines, and Apria Healthcare, reporting to seventeen managers. Over this period, Ed has had the good fortune of being recognized for working smart as he's been promoted four times, was awarded human resources Rookie of the Year in 2017 and Change Champion in 2018 at Ross Stores, Inc., appeared on the cover of a national human resources periodical, *Employee Benefit News*, in 2013 for work he performed at Hawaiian Airlines, and taught human resources courses at the University of California–Irvine from 2012 to 2018, where he was presented with the Distinguished Instructor Award in 2017.

He has presented human resources topics at major human resources association conferences, including HR Executive and WorldatWork, and served as a contributing editor to major human resources periodicals, including *Employee Benefit News* and *cfo.com.*

Ed has been appointed to advisory councils for major employers and human resources associations, including Anthem, Kaiser Permanente, and Wells Fargo.

Prior to entering the working world, Ed was a professional student as he earned a BS from Providence College, JD from Western New England University–School of Law, and an MBA from Auburn University. He is a licensed attorney in New Jersey.

When he's not trying to act like a human resources superhero, Ed lives in Dublin, California, and enjoys sports, traveling, exercising, and spending time with his wife, Christy, their three children, Sarah, Corinne, and Liam, and labradoodle, Alfie.

Visit Ed and all of the good stuff he's picked up in his human resource travels at www.edbraywrites.com.